The Power of Ignorance

The Power of
Ignorance

14 Steps To Using Your Ignorance
To Become Happier, Safer,
More Confident and More Likeable,
To Forget Your Limitations, Inspire Yourself
With Successes You've Never Had,
and Achieve Your Goals
In Addition To Enhancing
Your Ignorance To Promote
All Those Things, and
Well-Being Generally

by Vaguen
with Chris Gibbs & TJ Dawe

*Based on original material and characters
by Jeff Sumerel and Sam Reynolds*

BRINDLE
& GLASS

© Chris Gibbs and TJ Dawe 2006

All rights reserved. The use of any part of this publication reproduced, transmitted in any form or by any means, electronic, mechanical, recording or otherwise, or stored in a retrieval system, without the prior consent of the publisher is an infringement of the copyright law. In the case of photocopying or other reprographic copying of the material, a licence must be obtained from ACCESS the Canadian Reprography Collective before proceeding.

The Power of Ignorance name, characters, and original materials are the sole property of Spontaneous Productions, all rights reserved. For licensing agreements, more information or inquiries about The Power of Ignorance please visit www.powerofignorance.org or www.spontaneous.net or contact Vaguen@powerofignorance.org.

For more information on the stage production
visit www.tjdawe.com and www.chrisgibbs.ca

Library and Archives Canada Cataloguing in Publication
Dawe, T. J. (Ti-Jon David), 1974-
The power of ignorance : 14 steps to using your
ignorance / TJ Dawe & Chris Gibbs.

Spin-off humor book for the play of the same name.
ISBN 1-897142-13-7

1. Self-actualization (Psychology)--Humor. I. Gibbs, Chris, 1970-
II. Title.

PS8557.A84697P692 2006   C818'.602   C2006-902673-4

Cover photo: Mark Jackson, www.markjackson.ca
"You Make My Hips Buck" by Aaron Macri © 2003
All rights reserved. Used by permission.

Canada Council   Conseil des Arts
for the Arts   du Canada

Brindle & Glass is pleased to thank the Canada Council for the Arts and the Alberta Foundation for the Arts for their contributions to our publishing program.

Brindle & Glass is committed to protecting the environment and to the responsible use of natural resources. This book is printed on 100% post-consumer recycled and ancient-forest-friendly paper. For more information, please visit www.oldgrowthfree.com.

Brindle & Glass Publishing
www.brindleandglass.com

1 2 3 4 5 09 08 07 06

PRINTED AND BOUND IN CANADA

For Norman, but I'm not sure why.

*Alison,
the lone wolf,

Chris Gibbs.*

Preface to the First Introduction

Ladies and gentlemen of both sexes, welcome.

Just by opening this book on the Power of Ignorance, you have taken the first step on a journey—a journey of the *mind*.

The journey will be exciting, strange, and frightening, and not everyone will make it.

But you will not go alone. You will have a guide, a man who has shown countless before you how to tap into potential they never knew they had. A man named Vaguen.

That man is me.

Vaguen (me) has (have) helped thousands of people in the tens of thousands of seminars he has given all over the world.

?

As you read my words you may notice that my perception is very different from yours. You will undoubtedly ask yourselves, "What does this all mean?"; "Did he say what I think he said?"; "I don't understand!"

Well, if you don't understand, then you are *already using* your Power of Ignorance. Yes, *your* Power of Ignorance.

Ignorance.

Please turn the page (forward) and take the second step into the world of *Ignorance!*

The First Introduction
Why This Is NOT A Stupid Book

The Power Of... Ignorance!?

I'm sure your first reaction to the title of this book was to say, "*The Power of Ignorance*! This must be a joke!"

You may have felt disappointed or even angry that a publisher would soil the bookshelves with something so obviously pointless. Maybe you grabbed a copy off the shelf or table and demanded to see the manager of the store, angrily waving the book in the face of whoever came to deal with you.

You probably came back to the bookstore later that night and threw a brick at the window before vowing never ever to read again.

And you know what? Your reaction is perfectly understandable.

I'm sure if I'd been told twenty years ago that not only would I be the author of a book called *The Power of Ignorance*, but also have a very fulfilling career as a motivational speaker teaching people just that, I'd have been disbelieving too.

Context

... although that would really depend on context. If the person telling me this had been clad all in silver, appeared in a blaze of light, declared that they were from the future and had then proven that fact with a prediction which then came true—a long-shot winning an important horse-race for example—I'd believe what they were saying wholeheartedly. But if it had just been someone in a coffee-shop who'd brushed against me and then declared that the brief physical contact had allowed them a glimpse of the future, well then I'd take what they were saying with a very large grain of salt—the kind that doesn't occur naturally, but can only be cultivated in a lab!

Ignorance Is Bad.

Or Is It?

No.

Like most of us you have been taught that the key to success is knowledge. You've been taught that the pursuit of knowledge is somehow more admirable than the pursuit of ignorance. In fact, ignorance isn't even seen as something that needs pursuing!

Ignorance has been a dirty word. You probably went to a school where academic achievement was rewarded, and ignorance punished; you've watched game-shows on TV where people have won because of the things they knew, while those who knew less were pitied and probably mocked behind the scenes and snubbed at the after-show party; you've listened with bated breath, as we all do, to the announcement of each year's Nobel Prize winners and you've seen that they are always people who display intelligence and knowledge.

You've always *"known"* that knowledge is good, ignorance is bad.

You Think Too Much

And yet we also constantly hear phrases like "You think too much," "You're too smart for your own good," "Nobody likes a smartass," and "Have you seen *The Man Who Knew Too Much*? Good film isn't it?"

It's as if our subconsciousnesses understand what we do not—that there is a time for thinking, and a time for *not* thinking. That while there is much to be said for *re*flection, there is just as much to be said for *de*flection (of thought (i.e.—not thinking (hence *de*flection (of thought)))). That just as we have always recognized the power of knowledge, we must now embrace the Power of Ignorance.

What's My Point?

In my years as a motivational speaker, conducting seminars and workshops and helping people achieve their personal goals and realize their dreams, I have encountered thousands of men and women who were completely lost. Before they met me they were desperate for any kind of guidance and ready to turn to the first charlatan with a confident demeanour pushing any kind of "answer" that came along.

I've seen that in nearly every case, their problems could be traced to an over-reliance on knowledge, and the "benefits" that come from it. And by turning these people towards ignorance I have allowed them to achieve successes they never even knew they'd dreamt of.

Healthy Balance

Ignorance has changed lives for the better. It has already helped you in your own life, and it can help all of humanity. The real key to success is a healthy balance of knowledge and ignorance. An example I always like to give at my seminars is that you need to know enough about cars to be able to cross the road safely, but you also won't get very far if you have such a thirst for knowledge that you peer into their windshields as you're crossing, because you have to *know* what the inside looks like.

Because you'll get hit by the cars.

Usually with that parallel, I begin to see a look of confusion on the faces of my students. I'm sure you're confused too.

Good.

Confusion is the boulevard to ignorance.

Walk down that boulevard now.

Join the few who understand the importance of understanding that a lack of understanding is unimportant.

The First Step

By picking up this book you have taken the first step to unlocking your own Power of Ignorance. You have pushed aside this "knowledge" that ignorance is bad, and allowed yourself to *not know* whether it's bad or not. You have begun to give yourself one of the most important benefits of the Power of Ignorance. You've begun to give yourself the benefit . . . *of the doubt!*

The Second Introduction
Who Am I?

I am Vaguen, a living *and* breathing example of the Power of Ignorance.

I left university exactly twenty-five years and two months ago, dropping out after just eight years. I was armed only with an idea: that knowledge isn't good; and a purpose: helping others. While at university my greatest joy had been the feeling I had when I acted as an unofficial counsellor to the other students. They would tell me what was troubling them and I would listen, then I would tell them a story about my own life, something that I felt would illuminate their situation, and I'd suggest a possible solution to their problem. They would nearly always walk away realizing that they weren't as messed up as they thought they were. It made me very proud indeed.

Dream

It was while I was still at university that my dream of speaking to the world began to take shape, but the professors with whom I shared this dream told me it was ridiculous. They were very confident about this. In fact, they *knew that it would never happen* (italics mine).

I decided that I *didn't know that it would never happen* (italics mine too). And over their strenuous objections I left university and entered the great unknown. (Their objections to my leaving were so strenuous—often in a very physical way—that it reminded me of the strong first impressions I'd had of the university when I'd arrived. I had been sure it was some kind of facility for the insane into which my parents were placing me so they could live the life of ease and freedom they'd always wanted to! First impressions! An asylum! Ha ha ha!) (Ha!) (Ha!) (HAAAAAA!)

Inkling

At that point I had an inkling that knowledge wasn't *it*. But if not knowledge, what?

Through many encounters that I had with people in a wide variety of situations—people on buses; people getting off buses; people waiting for buses; people who had been left behind as the bus went past (left behind by buses)—I realized I was not alone. These wise men (and one of them might have been a woman) showed me that there was another world, a previously unknown—or "ig-known"—world of possibilities, a world accessible through the Power of Ignorance.

I immediately began travelling throughout the world, studying with Igmasters, striving to pay little or no attention to what they told me. I have reached levels where I never thought it would be possible. I am now very proud to say that I am a Master Ignoramus.

Seminars

On my return I began touring and giving seminars, promoting these ideas. In the beginning my seminars were very sparsely attended, and I'd be the first person to say that they weren't very good! Actually, they were so bad I probably wouldn't be the first person. I'd be the second! Or the third! Sometimes we'd run out of time before it got to my turn at all!

For years my talks would be greeted with stunned silence and shaking heads. I met other motivational speakers who told me that they *knew* that my ideas would *never help anyone or find an audience* (italics theirs). They *knew* that I didn't have enough life experience to make it work. Why would anyone care about my opinion?! Those speakers who had actually listened to what I had to say also *knew* that my message was fuzzy at best, ludicrous at worst. Even my pronounciation of certain words was fuel to their fire!

Thrown

Of course I was thrown by this. They were so confident, they'd done amazing things and had years of experience in this field, without a doubt they *knew* what worked and what didn't work.

But I refused to let go of my dream. I could see that this was a perfect time and a perfect way to prove what I was saying. I kept at it, reminding myself every day that I *didn't know* that my approach was doomed to failure, that I *didn't know* that every aspect of my attempts to be a successful motivational speaker was flawed, from my creased suit to my badly thought-out and often contradictory arguments, that I *didn't know* that I would never succeed in anything, because I just wasn't good enough.

Holding

You're holding this book in your hands, so you're probably saying, "I *know it's going to be ok*." (italics yours)

Some of you may be saying, "Oh, I wonder if it'll work out." If you're one of those people, *holding this published book in your hands* and wondering what the end of my story is, then you have no need of my guidance to the world of Ignorance.

Others amongst you may be saying, "No, Vaguen, don't give up! Pretty soon I'll turn the page, and I really want there to be writing there!" For those people, flip the page and take a look. Now flip back to here. See? I think you have your answer. (It worked out fine.) (No italics.)

I continued to tour my seminars and push my philosophy, and to use my own Power of Ignorance to help keep me going, confident that I would succeed because I *didn't know* how or why. After over nine and a half gruelling years of hard work, I began to notice a change in my audiences.

The Shaking

The shaking heads of disbelief at my observations gradually gave way to a reaction I hadn't expected: laughter. At first it would be a few laughs of recognition as people saw their own foibles so accurately pinpointed. Then they would laugh in sheer joy at how simple the insights that the Power of Ignorance gave could be. After a while that laughter would extend to the whole seminar, as the audience reacted with glee all the way through:

glee at the message I was giving them, glee at the potential that they saw opening up to them in their own lives. Glee, glee, glee!

As word of mouth spread my seminars became very well attended, and more and more people would laugh, showing me that I was getting through. They began to laugh even before I said anything, and long after they left. If they saw me on the street they would point and laugh too. Glee, glee, glee!

Unusual Venues

I became so successful that I found myself being booked to speak in places that didn't normally have motivational speakers: comedy clubs, theatres—even birthday parties—and my message would usually get an even warmer reception!

This tendency of people learning about the Power of Ignorance to react with laughter has lead to a little confusion. My experience with this book has been that those few places that actually stock it—those three bookstores and that library in Winnipeg—will actually make the mistake of putting it in the humour section! Please, if you're ever in a bookstore that stocks *The Power of Ignorance* (or that library) I would like to ask you now to take a copy from the humour section and place it in the self-help section where I truly believe it could help more people. Thank you.

Largest Pile

Those other motivational speakers had all *known* that I would fail. They had *known* that everything I was doing was wrong. But I *knew no such thing*. And now you're holding this book, my book, a book which often has the largest pile in those prestigious discount bookstores!

All the amazing success that I have is due to the Power of Ignorance: success that could be yours.

Remember: you don't know what isn't possible, therefore *anything* isn't possible.

The Third Introduction
Research

Misconception

"Why do I need to read a book on ignorance? Surely the best way to become ignorant is to not read anything!" is a comment I've heard often as I've written this book. It's the main reason I now write with the door closed.

This assumption makes "sense"—after all, aren't we constantly surrounded by ignorant people? (Well, I'm not, but people I talk to always refer to "that weirdo," an idiot who won't go away even at the most obvious hints, a sad loser who doesn't even know when he's being referred to!)

It is a point that will be repeated often throughout this book (as they all are) (except the points that aren't even made once) that ignorance is not something that happens automatically.

The attainment of a State of Ignorance is something that requires effort just like any other. You wouldn't expect to achieve enlightenment, sainthood, or daydreaming without work! Would you? Well?!

Research

As an Igmaster I had already accumulated a vast non-knowledge of ignorance, but I knew that to write this book I would have to take this one step further. I needed that little something *less*. So I worked. For years I gathered up every book on the subject I could get my hands on. I clipped out article after article, and combed through newspaper files and microfiches in dozens of libraries. I found countless essays on the subject in obscure periodicals and magazines. I gathered them all together and put them in a giant pile, and *didn't read them*. I ignored every single one of them. Let me tell you, it wasn't easy. But I was driven by my goal.

A Single Man

Soon this task proved too daunting for a single man. I hired an assistant. She uncovered even more books, articles, and essays, as well as novels, stories, poems, pamphlets, broadsides, photographs, folk songs, interview transcripts, charts, graphs, and unpublished graduate theses. She even came upon a relevant series of bumper stickers! Some of these materials she shredded, others she burned. Some she blotted out portions of with a thick black marker to remove any possibility of their being comprehended if I ever tried to read them. At the end of her work, she boarded a bus and never returned. Appropriately, I don't know where she went. Or what her name was. It didn't matter. I had important work to not do!

A Heading

With every item I didn't absorb I increased my ignorance. And only by catching a glimpse of how much information is out there (without reading it) can we begin to understand how ignorant we truly are.

It wasn't long before I hadn't read more source material than anyone else. Instead of being at the top of the mountain seeing everything, I was at the bottom of the valley, seeing nothing. And I was upside-down. Digging! At least I thought I was. It proved to be one of many, many myriads of things I didn't know. For how can a person know that he knows less than anyone else? How? HOW?

I have no idea. The crowning place in the field of ignorance is a humble position—one its bearer doesn't realize he or she has. It might be me. If I ever find out, I'll immediately lose it. But in the meantime, suffice it to say I've accumulated an incredible amount of material and ignored every letter and punctuation mark of it.

But not the spaces. I never ignored the spaces . . .

Summary

And that's why you should read a book about ignorance.

The Fourth Introduction
How To Use This Book

The main thrust of this book is contained in the thirteen steps that you will need to take to improve your life with the Power of Ignorance.

Each step will show you a tool or technique (or both) that you can use to make yourself successful, rich, fulfilled, or just plain happy (happier than now anyway).

They're copiously illustrated with examples—drawn from successful people, wealthy people, good-looking people, and people just like you.

The thirteen "steps" should be read in sequence, but you can do that in any order you please.

Hold On!

"But hang on!" you're saying. "You said thirteen steps! But there are more than thirteen chapters! What gives, man? I want answers!"

Well, okay.

Interspersed within and between these chapters there are essays, pictures, activities, and techniques that you can use that will help you to enhance your level of ignorance overall. And an enhanced level of ignorance will help with all the steps! And with everything else too!

Conventions

In order for you to get the most out of this book, you'll need to read it. I will use several conventions that I'll familiarize you with now.

Definition of Ignorance

At various times throughout the book, I'll be using the word "ignorance." You may have noticed I already have. It's a key word in understanding the Power of Ignorance—far more important than "of." The dictionary definition of "ignorance" is "Unwissenheit," but that tells us nothing. I have had to come up with my own definition. I have used "ignorance" to cover both the concept of *"not knowing"*—i.e. a lack of knowledge—and *"not thinking"*—i.e. a lack of thinking.

As you can see, from time to time I've used a dictionary in an attempt to help clarify a word's meaning. The dictionary that I use is the *Langenscheidts Schulworterbuch Englisch–Deutsch/Deutsch Englisch (3rd Edition)*.

Gender pronouns

For male people, when not referring to them by name, I have used the gender pronoun "he." For female people, "she." I have used the same convention to refer to animals whose gender is known. Otherwise the animal will be an "it." People whose gender is not known will be referred to as "he/she," unless they're within earshot, in which case I will use the term "your friend there" (if they came with someone I know) or "that person."

Things are all "it." Including cars. And boats.

?

Taking Notes

Nodding

As you're reading this book, you might find yourself nodding and saying things like "That's a good point" and "I sure do agree with that." At other times you might find a passage that resonates so strongly with you that you'd like to carry it around with you in your mind for the rest of your life. And at other times still you may come upon sentences you disagree with entirely. Or that you feel don't take an idea as far as you'd like to. And some points will be repeated. Several times.

You Bought It

Keep in mind this is your book. You bought it. It's yours to do with as you please. There is no one waiting to descend on you and give you a good thrashing and lock you in the cabinet under the sink if you write in it. Unless you're borrowing it.

So write in it. Take notes.

Ah!

"Ah!" but you might say. "How can I? There's very little empty space in it. You've taken all the choicest portions of each page for yourself, Mr. Vaguen." And you're right. I have. But not all of them. Look closely. There are the margins. There is the blank space between paragraphs. Like that lush white expanse above this one. There's considerable room between words. And then there are many letters in the English language which contain closed loops, such as the letter "O." Some people draw happy faces in that space. But a true ignoramus will make much better use of it.

Using revolutionary techniques like this one, how can you fail? Ignorance is practically guaranteed.

?

Absorbing Ignorance While You Sleep

Another way to use this book is to read it while you sleep.

Why do such a thing? I'll explain.

There used to be a physical reason why this was not possible, but now there isn't. Recently, scientists have discovered the means for you to stuff books straight into your head while you sleep.

Here's how to do it.

How To Do It

There are three ways.

Way One:

Put the book on your nightstand. Get into bed. Tuck yourself in. Good. Now pick up the book, open it to the first page. Place it on your face. Put your hands down by your side. Well done. Now go to sleep. Excellent. In the morning, wake up. Remove the book from your face. Place it back on the nightstand until you're ready to go to bed that night. Repeat this each night until you've reached the end of the book.

If you have trouble keeping the book in place, use glue or a leather strap.

Way Two:

Purchase the audio version of the book. It's more expensive, but that's preferable. Wait until you're sound asleep, and then put the tapes on your stereo. Press "play." Adjust the volume so it isn't playing loud enough to wake you up. Your unconscious ears will hear the words, even if your conscious ears can't hear a thing. Turn the tape from Side A to Side B whenever you need to. Change from the first tape to any of the others when necessary as well. As the sun gradually dawns, put the tapes back in their cases and turn off the stereo. Now it's time to wake up. Wake up. Good morning.

Employing these means, you should get through the book in one afternoon.

Result

By using any of these techniques, you'll receive the book straight into your subconsciousness mind, where it would have ended up anyway. You'll be ignorant, without knowing how or why, or anything else. And that's ignorance indeed. And you'll have saved yourself a great deal of valuable time.

You can use that surplus time to read the book.

Chapter 1
Preparing For The Journey

As has been mentioned, by reading this book you are embarking on a journey. This is a metaphorical journey, but just like a real one, it will require preparation. You wouldn't expect to travel to Denver, say, without preparing first, so why should a metaphorical journey be any different?

It's not.

In this chapter you will take all those mental steps that will prepare you for ignorance. You will pack your metaphorical bag, say goodbye to your metaphorical loved ones (and your mother) and make arrangements for someone to look after your metaphorical dog.

Embracing Ignorance

In our world there is much resistance to ignorance. The very term is fraught with negative associations. There are dozens—nay, hundreds—of schools throughout the world whose sole purpose is to increase their students' knowledge. But how many devoted to the removal of it?

No one knows.

By its very nature, the answer to that question is impossible to discover. But we may assume the number isn't incredibly high.

Because the tide is turned so strongly against us our first preparation, the most important one so far, is that we must embrace ignorance—fully, and unreservedly.

Emphatic

The best way to do this is to make a great, emphatic declaration. Preferably out loud, but in silence will do.

The important thing with such a declaration is it must be specific to *your* life, to *your* experience and to *your* concerns. To *you*. If *I* were to print *my* own declaration, *it* would be so rooted in the details of *my* life as to be well nigh inapplicable to all but a few of *you*.

Instead, *I*'ve written a Universal Declaration of the Embracement of Ignorance. *It*'s printed below.

Handy Note

Just a handy note—the blanks are not meant to be read as pauses, or as the word "blank." Or "line." Or, if reading the thing in your head—just to get the sense of it—as the syllable "hm." You're to fill in the blanks with actual words, tailored to you. You can even change them each time you read it, if there are multiple details for that blank in your life.

Here it is, on its own page.

I, _____ do stand here and let the world know that I welcome Ignorance into *my* life.

I am ready to release my hold on knowledge and allow the Power of Ignorance to help me _____, _____ and to attain _____.

Oh yes, there may be people who won't support me on this venture, like _____ or _____ or my _____, but it's my choice, and whether they're with me or not, I'm committed. Yes, even if they were to _____ me or call me a _____ or an_____, or a _____'s _____, my resolve would hardly waver at all. Not noticeably, anyway, to anyone but _____ or perhaps my pet ___.

All of my life people have filled me up with their own _____, telling me what to_____, where to_____ and what not to _____. Well ____ them! They've even threatened to have me declared _____ and throw me in a padded _____, feeding me nothing but _____ and gutter scrapings! Yeah! And they call themselves my _____?! If they really loved me then why all the _____s when I was a child? Why did I have to peel all those _____ and end up getting whacked with a wooden _____ no matter how many sacks I got through in an all nighter?

Oh, _____ _____ _ _____ __ _____ _____'_ _____!!! ___ _
___ _____-_____ _____ ___ _____ . _____ __ _ __ _____ ,
"_____" _____ ? _____ ___ _____ _____ _____
(or to put it another way, _____ __ _____) ___ _____
_____ _____ . ___!! _____ _____ _____ _____ .

A _____!!

Yes. One day their crumbly edifice of knowledge will _____. Yes it will. You watch. And I'll be there, standing _____ly on the pile of the bent, broken _____s of my _____s. And I'll be there, laughing in triumph because I, _____ am ig_____.

(Declaration ends here, stop emphatically reading out loud.)

Congratulations. You have now metaphorically packed your bag, which is like making yourself a packed lunch of simile sandwiches.

Wavering

There may be times when you feel yourself wavering, when you feel doubt creeping in. If you do find yourself analogistically hungry in this way, feel free to repeat the declaration, every hour if necessary. Louder each time. You'll find that the more you do this, the more all those people who want to tell you you're wrong will keep it to themselves. Those _____s.

?

Where You At

If you look at this book as a map, then somewhere on that map you will find the Land of Ignorance. By purchasing and/or reading this book you have taken *another* first step on your journey. You have bought the map.

But, as anyone who has ever tried to find something in a shopping mall could tell you, a map is useless to you without an arrow and the words "You Are Here."

With that in mind, before you set off to where you want to be, it is important for you to know where you are *right now*.

Questions

The questions that you will find over the next few pages will help you narrow down exactly where on the road to ignorance you are standing, and in which direction you're facing.

How long was the Hundred Years' War?

An opera is to a libretto as a steeplejack is to a _____.

What animal are the Canary Islands named after?

Complete this sequence: 1, B, car, Steven, _____, the concept of Time.

Which of the following does not belong?

List these numbers in order of preference: 19, 20, 15, 16

Are you bigger than a breadbox?

If A=1, decode this message: 1, 1, 1, 1, 1, 1, 1, 1, 1, 1, 18, 7, 8!!!

An orange is to a glass of juice as a basketball is to an _____.

List these numbers in order of preference: 4, 5, 3, 15, 4, 9, 14, 7

Who do you think you are?

A train is travelling at 40 mph. If it leaves Chicago at 7:00 pm, how soon will it get to Denver?

Think of a number between 1 and 10. Now multiply it by 9. Add the digits together. Subtract 5. Think of the letter of the alphabet that corresponds to that number. Think of a country that starts with that letter. Take the last letter of that country. Think of an animal whose name starts with that letter. Take the last letter of that animal. Think of a fruit whose name starts with that letter. Are you thinking of a dog eating a peach in Denver? I am.

List these numbers in order of preference: 20, 8, 5, 19, 5

How do you feel?

What is the biggest reason why we *shouldn't* hire you?

Why are maintenance hole covers round?

What common phrase is shown here:

MEA 11 FORM

------------------- ?

       Mr.

List these numbers in order of preference: 14, 21, 13, 2, 5, 18, 19

(For answers go to page 74)

For every correct answer, give yourself 4 points. Take your total score and multiply by 3 (are you sure you want to continue?). Add your age to this number, then subtract by a number that will total less than 37. In your local phone book, find the page that corresponds to your current total. Subtract or add the number 2 so that you end with a positive number. This number is *your* individual ignorance number.

？

Personality Types

Another way of finding where you are, equally important, is to discern what kind of personality you have.

We constantly hear people referring to those around them as "he's a real smarty-pants" or "look at that know-it-all" or "HE'S SO OPEN-MINDED!!!!"

There are an almost infinite number of ways that we can categorize other people and ourselves. In fact "other people and ourselves" is one of them. One of the most common, and the most useful for our purposes today is to place people into categories according to the different ways in which they approach their brains, their thinking resources, their knowledge and the knowledge of others.

Below you will find a list of some of these personality types and explanations of what is meant by them. I'm sure as you read them you'll recognize many of the people you know. You will also find yourself here.

The Smarty-pants

These people always have an answer for everything. They're very quick to volunteer information, or a solution to a problem, even if you haven't asked for it. Often when faced with someone else's failure, you'll hear them say things like, "Yes, I knew it wouldn't work." And "I wish you had come to me." They will greet any new knowledge with a nod, as if to say, "Yes, that confirms what I'd already thought." They can be useful, if some electrical appliance breaks down for instance, but mostly they're just annoying. As in that old saying, "No one likes a smarty-pants so go back to the cellar but keep the light off we're not made of money you naughty naughty brat. And no reading!"

The Know-It-All

The know-it-all is very similar to the smarty-pants, except that the know-it-all doesn't know as much.

The Open-Minded Man

Open minded people respect knowledge like beautiful noble nomadic folk of yore respected the wild cows that roamed the prairies. They live in a perfect balance with knowledge, neither rejecting nor restraining information. They welcome new knowledge when it comes, and let it go when newer knowledge replaces it. Often they can keep hold of several contradictory truths at once.

The Teacher

Teachers are very keen to push knowledge away, in every sense of the phrase. They are constantly trying to pass knowledge off to others, without keeping any for themselves. You can easily identify a teacher by their habit of telling you what books to read or how many times you have to run around that field. But don't try to tell them you need to go to the bathroom; they don't want to know!

The Child

People who are children combine the best aspects of open-minded people and smarty-pantses. They soak up knowledge like sponges, but are quick to throw it away if some more attractive knowledge comes their way. They are very inquisitive, but they shouldn't annoy mummy with their questions, she's got important things to do. That holiday's not going to plan itself!

The Dog

Dog-people are adorable. Like dogs.

The Scientist

Scientists are more interested in how the knowledge is obtained than whatever merits it may have. They will always be trying to verify what you're saying, to see how you came up with the conclusions that you've drawn. They are often cold-blooded and completely lacking a conscience.

The College Professor

These people are always trying to understand the world around them. They will constantly be asking questions, attempting, as they put it, "to get to the bottom of things." They believe there is no question that can't be answered, no puzzle that can't be solved. And for some reason, even though they're the professors and you're the student, they'll try to get you to come up with the answers: "Well, why do you believe you're at *university?*"

The Mother

The mother's attitude to knowledge is complex. She will often react angrily to simple childish inquisitiveness, and will belittle any knowledge that the child might learn elsewhere. She never admits to not knowing anything, and if a childish innocent were to make the mistake of showing her exactly where in the book it contradicts what she's said, she's quick to tear up his library card, and have herself "a good ol' book burnin' in the yard!"

The Heartbreaker

The heartbreaker's attitude to knowledge is complex. She will often react angrily to simple childish inquisitiveness, and will belittle any knowledge that anyone might learn elsewhere. She never admits to not knowing anything, and if a childish innocent were to make the mistake of showing her exactly where in the book it contradicts what she's said, she's quick to tear up his library card, and have herself "a good ol' book burnin' in the yard!"

The Dream Woman

The dream woman is so called because that's the only place she exists. But if she did exist in real life she would be someone who *enjoys life*, who's not afraid to give of herself, and is appreciative of other people giving of themselves. She would see the good in others, and others would be better just for knowing her. She'd also have long brown hair.

The Life-Changing Guru

The life-changing guru is someone who helps others. He sees other people's pain and tries to help because he knows what pain is. His journey is a long and unintentionally solitary one. But when it isn't solitary, for some reason it's a whole lot worse.

?

Summary

By preparing for your journey you have completed the first step. Yes, I realize that taking the first step of a journey is something that's best done *after* the preparation, but as this is a metaphorical journey, the preparation can be considered a step in and of itself. And it should definitely be the first one. Even though you haven't actually gone anywhere. Because you won't. It's a metaphor.

Enhancing Your Ignorance Through Simple Everyday Activities

Changing to ignorance is a matter of reshaping habits.

I know we all fear change, the way a rabbit fears the top hat, but you needn't be intimidated. The steps are simple.

> 1. Firstly, set aside a quiet part of your house or apartment for ignorant contemplation.

Don't worry, you don't need to set up a little shrine and burn incense like a loony! On the other hand, if you wanted to, there'd be nothing wrong with that.

> 2. Next, focus on a simple phrase of your own devising.

Now, you certainly don't have to hum and chant and play a hand drum like some nitwit. But if you care to, that'd be an absolutely valid choice, fully approved of by any Igmaster.

> 3. Now repeat your phrase a good number of times.

Rest assured, you don't have to do it out loud and irritate everyone in the neighbourhood. Then again, if it suits you to, then scream away. There are many strong-voiced members in the flock of ignorance.

> 4. Initiate a simple physical sequence of your choice.

It can be as simple as the extension of a single finger. There's no need to fear I'm going to tell you to do an elaborate dance with spins, kicks and flailing arms, like some unnatural freak—but, if you're inclined in that direction, by all means, twirl like a propeller. That'd be a perfectly acceptable choice.

> 5. Finally, combine the physical sequence and the repeating of the phrase—but do so without thinking about either one.

You don't have to spend hours, or even weeks locked in this state like an absurd idiot—then again, if you do, that's fine. Even recommended.

Ignore all attempts to make you stop by the jealous "thinky" people in your life. They think they know what they're doing, while you don't think you don't know. Or will try not to. Especially if you're repeating your phrase and your physical activity at a sufficiently rapid rate and volume.

Cultivate these simple ignorance-enhancing habits into the fabric of your daily life. Spend time at them every day, no matter what else you have to do. You will know glorious results.

"Results of what kind?" you might ask. I haven't the slightest idea. I don't do these things.

Medical Student

A year ago, a young man who had attended one of my seminars came up to me and told me how much trouble he was having in medical school.

"Please," he implored me, "Being a doctor is my life's dream. How could I have known it would be hard? Tell me how the Power of Ignorance can get me through Med School."

So I did.

"Medical science is all about Ignorance. Think of the thousands of biological processes which occur within the human body every week without any of us being aware of them. Think of how many seriously ill people are deliberately kept in the dark about how hopeless their situations really are, thereby sparing them and their doctors undue awkwardness. Think of the high salaries doctors can charge because no one knows that nurses do all the work. Think of the millions successfully treated every day with placebos. In fact, in some European countries, the mother will actually eat the placebo after the baby is born."

"So here's what you do with your bad medical school grades," I said. "Ignore them."

Exactly That

That young man did exactly that. And just six weeks later, he was expelled.

He took up calligraphy.

He's now very happy as a practising doctor—with some very nice looking diplomas.

I'm told he's helped put an end to a lot of people's suffering.

Chapter 2
Accepting The Ignorance You Already Have

The road to ignorance, on which you are embarked, is a long one. And a long journey can be daunting. But you can take encouragement from this: part of you is already there.

That's so important, I'm going to repeat it in italics.

Part of you is already there.

Imagine yourself on a train going from London to Brighton. Wouldn't the journey be easier if you suddenly realized that your pancreas, your left leg and your skull were already in Brighton, waiting for you at the station?

Well, no it wouldn't. But you'd be less likely to change your mind and go somewhere else.

Ignorance Is Pervasive

Ignorance is pervasive in our world and our lives, it just isn't always called "ignorance."

You have already used and allowed ignorance to benefit you and your life in a number of ways, without even knowing it, for instance . . .

Breathing

I think I can say without fear of contradiction that everyone reading this right now is breathing.

I think I can also say, also without fear of contradiction, that at least 75 percent of you have not been actively thinking about your breathing the entire time.

And yet not a single one of you has asphyxiated or fainted.

Remarkable, isn't it?

Yes it is.

Breathing—the very water of life—has been in the hands of your Inner Ignorance this whole time, and has been doing just fine.

But here's the truly salient point: if you were to actively pay attention to your breathing it would be substantially less effective. It might even stop altogether.

Thinking About Breathing

You're thinking about your breathing now aren't you?

Careful.

Unfortunately, by drawing your attention to this phenomenon, I have placed your breathing under your conscious control, endangering all of your lives.

I apologize, it seemed important.

YOU MAKE MY HIPS BUCK BABY
GIRL YOU DRIVE ME CRAZY
MY THIGHS ARE ON FIRE
AND I GOT A CRAMP IN MY SIDE

I've just quoted from boy-band supergroup Boygroove's wonderful piece, "You Make My Hips Buck."

I did this to distract your attention from thinking about your breathing, thus allowing you to breathe ignorantly once again, averting a mass death by suffocation, saving the lives of the millions who are reading this book, right now.

It worked, didn't it?

You're welcome.

Healthy Ignorance

This is just one of the many tools and techniques that we Igmasters can use to return ourselves and others to a state of healthy ignorance.

How it worked was, for those few brief seconds, you stopped thinking "inhale, outhale" and instead you thought, "Dig it! That sure is a grooooooovy tune!"

Unfortunately, by explaining the technique to you, I have returned the topic of this book to *breathing*, placing you all back in jeopardy. I apologize again.

If I do have to use the technique a second time, I won't explain why.

> IT AIN'T MUCH FURTHER TO MY CAR NOW PUDDIN
> I'LL MAKE YOU WANNA DO THINGS THAT YOUR MAMA SAID YOU SHOULDN'T
> SO GET CLOSE WITH ME MUFFIN
> WE'LL CLOSE THE KITCHEN DOOR AND THEN WE CAN START STUFFIN

I just quoted from that Boygroove song, *for no reason whatsoever.*

?

Sleeping

I think I can say without fear of contradiction that you all at some point sleep.

What purpose does sleep serve? Medical science admits—as do many medical scientists—that there's no explanation as to why human beings lapse into a benign coma every night. Or why they get so cranky when sleep is denied them, using nothing but ammoniated water and a poke from a large stick.

We don't need to learn how to sleep, either. Even the youngest of babies do it all on their own, needing only relative quiet, darkness, a comfortable surface, a blanket, a soft pillow, a full belly, and few sharp slaps to send them into a deep, satisfying slumber. The same can be said of primitive people the world over.

Sharks

And consider this: sharks don't sleep. Ever. Nor owls. Or those stupid crickets. In fact no animals do except dogs—the most advanced animal. Curled up on the bed and keeping our feet warm, twitching every now and then, and waking up to lick herself.

What does this tell us? That as a species strives into the land of thought, Nature pulls it back to where it belongs—that world of fantasy, colours and giant gaping peaches made of human flesh that we call the "dreamland"—in a word, to the universal sphere of Ignorance. In sleep we all have the Power of Ignorance.

Falling

If you concentrate on falling asleep, you can't. In fact, you can lose an entire night's sleep if you have *something on your mind*. (Not to be confused with having something on your *head*) (having something on your head is fine, and while it can interfere with your sleep if it's something like a rock or a car, for instance, it need not. In fact, if the something is a pillow, held there by a fellow university student it can actually help!)

As mentioned before, (one of many points that will be repeated throughout the book) sleep is nature's way of ensuring that we spend at least eleven hours a night in the land of ignorance.

Contrary to Nature

Thinking goes contrary to nature. Yes. Mountains don't think. Nor trees. Nor children. And humans only began to do so in the last few hundred years (depending on when you're reading this).

Every night our bodies send a message to our heads saying "Too much thinking!" which shuts us down for eleven hours, (fifteen in Newfoundland) no matter what we happen to be doing.

When we wake up in the morning, our minds are sluggish, and resist thought as much as possible until jolted by a powerful stimulant, such as coffee, tobacco, or electricity. And in most cases these substances aren't secreted from our bodies. No. We have to go get them.

As we can see, the thoughtlessness of sleeping is our natural state, but the thoughtfulness of waking can only be achieved with artificial means.

Marathon Stretches

Also bear in mind that people who go for marathon stretches without sleep go immediately and irreversibly insane. They stop thinking forever and are much happier for it.

Try it!

Captured soldiers are routinely brainwashed and reprogrammed using the same technique, and similarly, when released back into the world find they enjoy a much greater sense of purpose than they ever had before.

Religions work in the same way. If you've ever attended a 72-hour Group Prayer & Scream you'll know what I mean!

Those Presbyterians!!

The same goes for month-long jumping contests.

Nightly Excursions

So as you revel in your nightly excursions into deep states of unconsciousness, you should realize that what you are really enjoying is a good night's ignorance.

?

Communing with Infinity

Once again, I think I can say without fear of contradiction, that you don't know at least one thing. Possibly more.

Let me repeat that: "Don't know one thing. Or possibly more."

Whether that one thing you don't know is the Sanskrit word for "bashful" or the Hebrew word for "grumpy" or the Latin word for "aqueduct," we can all think of at least one thing that we don't know.

These are things we *know* we *don't know*.

Now, this might appear confusing, but it is followable. Like that figure-eight strip upon which ants walk, which turns out to only have one side. A long, single, twisting side, shaped over itself into a figure eight. A highway for disappointed ants who'd probably been promised food at the "end" of the track. How long would it take them to discern that they'd been tricked? After all, they are just ants. I don't know. You see, that right there is one thing I *know* I *don't know*! You can probably say the same thing about yourself. Unless you're an ant!

Unlike that strip, there is food at the end of this figure eight—big luscious dripping pink chunks of ignorance, which any ant would be delighted to endlessly pursue.

Returning

So returning to our thesis, we can probably all admit that there are things we don't know. And that this is normal and that we're aware of it.

So far so good.

But what about things we *don't know* we *don't know*? What about the answers to questions that we or anyone have never dreamed up?

Before the invention of the typewriter people didn't bemoan the difficulty of writing with a chisel and granite tablet. They didn't know it could be any easier. There weren't that many things to write about back then anyway.

Teasing

Imagine travelling back in time. It would be easy to tease the people you met in previous ages about their lack of prescription drugs, or rubber tires, or their inability to speak or understand proper English. But they wouldn't know what you were talking about. They wouldn't even begin to appreciate the things we take for granted that simply were not a part of their lives.

Now imagine someone from the future travelling back to our present age. It would be just as easy for them to poke fun at us about our lack of ability to travel through time or our non-shiny clothing. And we'd be similarly baffled by their teasings.

You see, we can never fully *know* what we *don't know*.

Only generations of the distant future will be able to look on us with loving pity for the multitude of things of which we have simply no idea.

As generations even further into the future will do with them.

And ones even further still will do with them.

And so on.

Can Never Be Eliminated

Ignorance is a constant in human experience. By its very nature it can never be eliminated.

We don't—and can't—*know* what we *don't know*.

We are *ignorant* of our *ignorance*.

Or—we are *very ignorant*. Of our *very ignorance*.

This is called "ignorance squared."

And once ignorance becomes squared it immediately cubes itself. Because if you were *ignorant* of your own *ignorance*, then there's certainly no way that you weren't *ignorant* of your *ignorance* of your *ignorance*.

And ignorant of *that*.

And *ignorant* of that.

And so on.

Infinitesimal Union

Without you even having done anything your ignorance multiplies itself logarithmically until it reaches an infinitesimal union with infinity.

Yes, that's right. Harnessing the power of your own ignorance is a communion with infinity. And who wouldn't want that?

Positive and Negative

As mentioned elsewhere in this book, the human brain, and, by extension, human beings, contain(s) a mixture of energy—some positive, some negative. We can probably look on our lives and see the interplay of these forces. Understanding how intertwined they are is fundamental to your development. You will need to look at positivity and negativism in your life. Here's what to do:

• First make a list of three positive things in your life. Characteristics you have, accomplishments you've accomplished, joyous moments, compliments received, chores completed, or even favourite foods. Write this list in longhand, on a sheet of paper.

If you can't come up with enough, don't worry. Fewer than three items will do. Or make some up.

• Take this list, and—without reading it—burn it. Hide the ashes. Don't mention to anyone that you've made such a list. This is essential. Try to forget having written it.

• Now make a list of two hundred negative things in your life. Broken dreams, unfulfilled potentials, character flaws, unrealized ambitions, bad grades, mistakes, disappointments, rejections, humiliations, accidents, spirit crushing moments, insults received, injuries, errors in judgment, inappropriate comments, social blunders, extended periods of loneliness and/or boredom, unhappy trips to the zoo, instances of bad luck, unsatisfying bouts of self abuse, differences between your hopes for yourself and the pathetic reality, instances in which you've tripped in public and gone sprawling onto the pavement, yelling wildly and standing up with a vast tear in your clothes.

Need more? How about a drawing of your own silhouette. Or a list of romantic possibilities who haven't been interested in you in the slightest and never will be. Or how about just the way people look at you, huh? How about that?

If you need more paper, go and get it. There's time. If your pen runs out of ink, replace it. If you find two hundred too limiting, surpass it. Leave it behind in the distance.

Now take this list, and stick it to your refrigerator door. Take it back down. Photocopy it. Enlarge it. Tack one up in your cubicle at work. Put one on the inside door of your locker. Keep one on you at all times for quick reference. Send yourself one in the mail, with a fake return name and address so that you trick yourself and won't recognize it until you open it. Read it before you go to bed at night. The formalization of this routine mental activity into a list will be very satisfying.

Nothing New

Now, ignorance is nothing new. Human beings have realized the value of ignorance since before the first caveman fell down from the trees. Into a cave.

Ignorance planted its seed in the fertile ground of the human mind and has done nothing but grow. We can find fragments of this ignorance in philosophies from all over the world. Let us first consider Western philosophy.

Millions Of Years

Millions and millions of years ago, in ancient Greece, Socrates said, *"True wisdom lies in knowing what you don't know."*
I couldn't have put it better myself. Because I don't speak Greek.

Ralph Waldo Emerson said, *"To be great is to be misunderstood."*
I don't know what he meant, but he was a great man.

Jesus Humphrey Christ said, *"Father forgive them, they know not what they do."*
"know not," pretty similar to ...
"not know"
Think about that.

Or don't.

As we can see, all of Western civilization has been squirted from the loins of ignorance.

Glorious Ends

But think about this.
All three of the great Ignorami I just mentioned came to glorious ends.
Socrates was forced to drink a cup of poisonous hemlocks.
Jesus was crucified.
And Ralph "Waldo" Emerson disappeared into a large crowd of people, and has never been seen again.

Eastern Philosophy

Let us now turn 360 degrees to look from Western to Eastern philosophy. The highest goal of Buddhism is to think about nothing.

That's so important I'm going to repeat it in italics.

To think about nothing

In fact, it's so important I'm going to repeat it in *Italian*.

Pensare a niente

And italics.

But How?

To achieve this Buddhist sages have their apprentices ponder unanswerable questions, like, "What is the sound of one hand clapping?"

With the Power of Ignorance, every question is an unanswerable question. The Power of Ignorance allows us to ask ourselves, "What is the sound of two hands clapping?" and not even be able to venture a guess.

Chapter 3
Say "No!" To Knowledge

People often look back on their pasts and say "If I knew then what I know now . . ."

They rarely complete the sentence. They generally just let it trail off like that. And sit there gently nodding, eventually shedding a single self-pitying tear.

With this fragment they imply that they would have made better decisions with the knowledge accumulated in the ensuing years, and therefore would have led better lives.

But how often do we hear people say the opposite? When was the last time you heard someone look back on themselves and say "My lack of knowledge was exactly what I needed. If not for that, I'd be in dire shape."

Never.

Until now.

Thousands

Pick up any self-help book, (apart from this one) and you will find thousands of true stories of people who have used their knowledge to achieve success. It's easy to come away with the impression that that's the only way to do it! But we shouldn't ignore the dozens of people whose very *ignorance* was the key factor in the fulfillment of *their* dreams.

In this chapter we'll look at exactly that, examining several case histories of ignorance triumphant, and exploring how ignorance turns potential disaster into victory *every time*.

I'd like to start with an example from my own life.

An Example From My Own Life

When I was a younger man I was approached by a bespectacled young entrepreneur. I have to preserve his anonymity so I'll call him "Bob" Gates.

When Bob approached me he was at the end of his tether. "I haven't been able to get anyone to believe in me!", he said, "And frankly, if I get one more rejection I'm giving up! And people don't just reject me, they mock me and my unswaying commitment to fair business practices! And it really hurts my feelings!"

Bob was trying to find investors for his new electric computer machines. He explained his plan to me quite stridently, fervent in his belief that these new devices were "the way of the future."

All I had to do was send him my agreement and my investment money, and I'd be in on the first floor. The one on the ground.

It sounded good to me. Keep in mind these were innocent times. There was a widespread belief that as the years passed "technology" would become important.

I looked Bob straight in the eye and told him, "I believe in you."

"Thank you," said Bob, in an emotional whisper. "*Thank you.*"

My Money

Later, I gathered my money, counted it, smoothed it out, and fed the ends of the bills into one of the fax machines that were becoming more and more popular at this time. I dialed, got through and the money began to disappear. "Future, here I come!" said I . . . or so I thought . . . you see, it wasn't long before my money just rolled out the other side of the fax machine! What was going on?! I quickly checked and saw that all the serial numbers were the same! The only conclusion I could draw was that Bob had returned my money! Had he given up? I couldn't let that happen so I tried again, first sending a note that said, "I'm trying to show you just how much I believe in you!" But my money came back again.

I kept at it for an hour, but the result never varied.

Bob's Response

Bob phoned me later, angrily asking why I was doing this to him.

I explained that he should see that my actions showed exactly how I felt about him. He shouted at me that because of me he would never give up, that now he would trample unprincipled over the backs of anyone to get what he wanted.

At first I was disappointed. If only I'd *known* how to explain myself to Bob, I'd have been on my way to being a rich man.

But as the years went by I realized it was my ignorance that had saved me from what would have been a costly mistake.

Because who's ever heard of Bob Gates now??

?

Ignorance and the Art of Playing Poker

Imagine you're sitting at a table with four other men. Imagine you're a man, if you aren't one in the first place. One of the men thoroughly shuffles a deck of ordinary playing cards. He then deals five cards to each person, including him or herself. They all pick up their cards.

You would certainly hold your cards in such a way that you could see what their values are. But consider this: cards are only printed on one side. The other sides are completely blank, apart from a border around the edges, and an intricate swirling red or blue pattern. Or a picture of puppies.

Given this arrangement, *you* are able to tell the value of *your* cards, but someone sitting across from you can *not*. The game hinges on *their* ignorance of *your* cards.

You don't know what the other players have, and they don't know what you have. In fact, if you can suppress any emotional reaction to the goodness or badness of your cards, you can bluff them into thinking a good hand is actually a bad one, or that a bad hand is a good one. This technique is called "tricking."

But what of the face's unintentional colourings, twitches and sudden distortions that subtly give us away? How can we overcome that?

There is only one way: Ignorance.

Two Options

You have two options.

Your first option is to not know the rules of poker in the first place. If all of your cards, no matter what their value, mean as little to you as if they were written in Chinese, you won't react. Unless you're Chinese.

But even then, wouldn't you still be able to discern a few basic patterns? And really, how can one truly know nothing at all about the rules of such a common game? Doesn't one unintentionally absorb simple rudiments, such as "tens are worth more than threes," "aces are always high," or "In the hand with a One Eyed Jack the Two Eyed Jack is King"? Yes. Or at least if you hadn't, you have now. I apologize.

So we must then turn to technique number two.

Don't Look

Don't look at your cards—at all. You will only be able to maintain an unreadable composure if you genuinely don't know their value. Although you must convey the illusion that you do.

But how? Simple. Hold the cards backwards. Stare at the swirling patterns or beautiful puppies. Rearrange them meaningfully. Squint. Perhaps feign surprise, or disappointment. Nod your head, especially if you notice any of the other players looking in your direction in a studying manner.

Your tricking will be unparalleled. The other players will soon learn that your expression gives nothing away. And they won't even bother looking at your face at all!

What If I Don't Play Poker?

This principle can be applied in many non-poker-game situations.

A man once came up to me during one of my seminars and told me the following story:

> I was a top negotiator for a large company which
> was involved in a bidding war for a lucrative civic

construction contract. I knew that my performance at the negotiating table would either win or lose this important work for my company. The practicalities of the matter played a negligible part. They always do. I wasn't even certain what the contract was for!

As the talks were about to begin a secretary appeared saying she had an important message for me.

Knowing that all eyes were on me, I dismissed the secretary, with a pointed finger and a thrust arm gesture of almost Biblical proportions, saying 'Not until after I've signed this contract!' I could tell that my words, actions and the confidence that they'd shown had had the desired effect on the people in the room.

She left the message folded up on my briefcase and skulked out.

I negotiated as I had never negotiated before. I was eloquent, irritating, persuasive, pathetic, illogical, charming and bullying. I spoke as if the contract was mine by divine right. And even though my company's bid and reputation were less than good, I *won that contract*.

After the meeting I opened the message. I'd been fired.

That Man

Would that man have negotiated so well if he'd known he'd been turfed before the talks? Would he have won that contract? Well?

Answer me, reader! I know you're there!

Well OK, I'll tell you. He wouldn't. I know this because he finished his story by telling me that after he found out he was fired he called the city and blew the whistle on his now ex-employers, describing a series of made-up nefarious dealings. The city took the contract away and, disillusioned with the bigger companies, gave it to a much smaller firm.

You see, what we don't know can be our greatest asset. Especially when what we don't know is something really bad.

?

The Bank of Ignorance & The Bank Of Knowledge

Here's a true story told to me by two men after two of my seminars. It's actually two stories, but they're related, so I'll tell them one after the other, which will preserve the fact that they're two separate stories, although play up the similarities between them.

The Smarty-pants Banker

A man worked at a bank. He started as a teller, and from his first day on the job showed exceptional promise. He understood numbers. He could manipulate money as a concert pianist does the keyboard. When confronted with an unusual case, he found his head in a state of perfect clarity.

One day he received a summons to his boss's office. He was being given a promotion, he found out. Starting the following Monday he would make a leap in responsibility, autonomy, income, and prestige. He'd now be investing the bank's money. He received his own office in a high-rise tower and had a secretary.

Three days into the next week the man scheduled a meeting with his old boss and told him how happy he was in this new job. He felt perfectly suited to it. He knew what he was doing, and that was a good feeling.

The boss leapt up at that point and said "That's exactly why you've been promoted!" The man smiled at him. "We want you for your knowledge. For that great financial brain of yours. For your knack and intuition. For your infallible dexterity with numbers. Why, with what you know, you'll see things that lesser, dumber investors can't figure out. Your intelligence is your greatest asset to this company. And to yourself."

Armed with this vote of confidence, he charged into his new job investing with verve. He understood the fluctuations of the market and made nothing but wise decisions. He even made choices others secretly termed as "unorthodox," "risky" and "insane." Yet these moves reaped untold profits for his company. Things couldn't have been going better for him.

But, due to a sudden, massive, unexplainable downturn in the stock market, his bank lost everything and declared bankruptcy. The man was fired.

Knowledge had failed

Knowledge had failed.

The Ignorant Banker

Another man worked at another bank. He'd started in an entry-level position as a teller and from his first day on the job, showed no outstanding qualities of any kind. He had an average relationship with numbers, money, and customers—perhaps even lower than average. When confronted with an unusual case he found his head in a state of thick fog.

One day he received a summons to his boss's office. He was being given a promotion, he found out. Starting the following Monday he would make a leap in responsibility, autonomy, income, and prestige. He'd now be investing the bank's money. He received his own office in a high-rise tower and had a secretary.

Three days into his new job the man scheduled a meeting with his old boss and confessed to him that he was on the point of resigning. He didn't feel qualified for this new position. He didn't understand it. He didn't know what he could and couldn't do.

The boss leapt up and said "That's exactly why you've been promoted! I don't want you for your knowledge—I want you for your *ignorance*. You said it yourself—you don't know what you can and can't do. So you're not going to do the same things as everyone else. You won't make the same assumptions, and you won't be limited by the common consensus—which may or may not be right. It's your ignorance that gives you the clarity of vision to see what others might miss. Your ignorance is your greatest asset to this company. And to yourself."

From that point on he threw himself into his new job, investing the bank's customers' money with confidence and unfettered by what everyone else assumed was how things should be done.

Then, due to a massive, sudden, and unexplainable upturn in the stock market, his investments made some money.

The man kept his job.

Ignorance Had Triumphed

Ignorance had triumphed.

So answer me this, "reader": which bank would you rather invest in? Hmm? Well? Yes, that's right.

Questions

If you've made it this far into the book, you very possibly have some questions. Some of them will be answered in subsequent passages. Some will not. In either case, here's your chance to ask questions directly to me, Vaguen.

Think of your question.

Write it down.

Now ask it of me, out loud.

Keep in mind I can't hear you.

Repeat the question, please.

My answer to you is "I don't know."

You see, my Power of Ignorance allows me to answer any question appropriately and correctly, not only if I don't know the answer, but even if I don't know the question.

The answer is always either "I don't know" or "Denver."

The Plaque

As you pursue your own Power of Ignorance, of course, there will be times when you begin to doubt its benefits. As you get better and better at the lessons you'll learn here, you'll actually find that you will not only doubt their worth, you'll forget why you ever thought there was any.

It can be useful to have a reminder of why you are on this life-changing path. Now I realize this may seem like a contradiction, and yes it does. Surely the Power of Ignorance shouldn't need any reminders, aren't reminders the same as knowledge?

No they're not. A reminder is an **external** point of reference, knowledge *outside* your mind; that allows for complete ignorance *inside* your mind, where it's most important.

Example

Perhaps the best example is one that I use myself.

As I sit at my desk and write, I always smile when I look up at the wall above it and see the words;

> **Better the devil you know?**
> **Better the angel you *don't* know.**

I call it my "plaque." But really it's just too homemade for that worthy title. I'm not a carpenter, after all! The words, "better the devil you know" come from a record album cover that hangs from a nail. The question mark, and the second line are scratched into the wall using a butter-knife.

I find it incredibly useful to be able to look up at this plaque while I'm working at my desk, or I can look over at it while I'm cooking. Sometimes lying in bed I'll stare at it as I fall asleep, or I might glance at it when I'm standing by my shelf.

It serves as a constant reminder that the Power of Ignorance can be a way of dreaming big dreams, of never settling for second-best, but of always pushing away what you don't want in search for something better. Yes, you don't know what's behind the other door, but no one ever achieved happiness through settling for something they didn't like.

Copy It!

Feel free to copy my reminder if you want to, or find a different quote somewhere else in this book if it works better for you. I would advise against coming up with your own though, since you might accidentally stumble on a phrase that makes the Power of Ignorance sound like the ravings of a denial-crazed madman!

Chapter 4
Choose Ignorance And Be Happier

The Most Ignorant Time Of The Year

I'd like you now to think back to your childhood, and specifically to one of the happiest times of the year: Christmas, or if you don't celebrate Christmas, then whatever holiday you do celebrate where you see presents wrapped up under a tree for some time, but you're not allowed to open them.

Remember when you saw those presents, how happy you were? Remember the state of excitement you'd get into, wondering what they were? In fact, you probably spent weeks getting the most incredible joy from all the possible presents that could be in that wrapping paper!

Remember how you would ask your parents what was in there and their reply of "Wait and see!!" would make you even more excited. And they'd tease you and pretend that they were going to tell you after all, "Well, alright then, it's a . . . Oh no you don't, you nearly got me to tell you, and ruined your surprise! You little scamp!" And then their jokingly wagging fingers would straighten, wouldn't they, and their hands would come back ready for a full backhand slap. Remember that?

More Happiness

If you really think about it, you got more happiness from those presents when you didn't know what they were, than you did when you knew.

Wondering what was inside that brightly-coloured paper was even better than tearing it away, and finding out that your parents had given you a bag of cabbages, half a pack of pencils, or a clump of magic dirt. Wasn't it?

Even a present you liked, and were allowed to keep—like the

magic dirt—was more fun because of the anticipation of the day it would turn into a puppy, as your parents had promised you it would. Waking each day for three months and wondering—or to put it another way—*not knowing*—if today was the day, was much better than when the dirt was finally taken away by your parents, who told you, "I guess you just didn't want it to turn into a puppy badly enough."

Wasn't it though?

Eh?

Disneyland

Or remember how you felt when your parents said "We're going to Disneyland!" and you spent the most exciting four weeks imagining what it would be like.

Every day your parents would say "Only twenty more days before we go to Disneyland!" and then "Only nineteen days to Disneyland!"

Wasn't all that excitement better than when the day finally came and they asked "Why have you packed your bag?"

"Because we're going to Disneyland."

"Awwwwww, poor little fella. You misunderstood Mummy and Daddy. *We're* going to Disneyland. *You* obviously didn't want to go badly enough or you'd have bought yourself a ticket. Mummy and Daddy bought themselves tickets with the money they made *working*."

I think we all remember how disappointing it was every time that happened!

Magician

Or how about when you went to see a magician who did tricks—*magic* tricks.

Wasn't it better when you didn't know how the tricks worked? Didn't you prefer the world when you still believed magic existed—when you had no idea where the cute little rabbit went when the magician made him disappear into his scary top hat?

Wasn't that better than when your parents told you how it

worked, about how the hat was fitted with a hidden blender, and how the rabbit didn't really "disappear" at all, but was actually sliced into tiny pieces at the bottom of the hat and its little rabbit soul then went to Rabbit Hell, where it was forced to dance *naked* in front of a big, fat rabbit with no hair, until that bald rabbit tired of it whereupon it would be dropped into a pit where it would spend the rest of eternity tied to a rack and every time a little smarty-pants boy in the real world annoyed his parents by asking a question about something the rabbit would be stretched until it screamed in pain.

Wasn't your life better when you didn't know this?

Happiness From Ignorance

Those are just three examples from your own life where you have derived happiness from your own ignorance, but there are many more.

How many people's lives are temporarily brightened by hope between the time when they buy a lottery ticket and when they find out they haven't won?

How often have you watched someone's face light up as they imagine what they would do with their winnings?

Would you want to be the one to take that away from them? Would you want to be the one who says "Look! The odds of you winning this are 1 in over 83 *billion!* And that's U.S. billions! That means you have pretty much the same chance of winning whether you buy a ticket or not! And you *KNOW* this! And you're still playing! How much money have you lost on this over the years? Oh, I've had enough. Get out of my sight!"

If everyone who ever dreamed of winning the lottery, but never won, knew they weren't going to win, then there would be a lot less happiness in the world.

And the jackpots would obviously be much smaller too, so even the people who did win—which would be all of them—would lose money on each ticket. Imagine a world where people said, "If this lottery ticket wins I'm going to buy a cup of coffee. But not a latte."

You've just imagined a world without ignorance.

?

The Happiest Man on the Bus

Look at that man sitting on the bus, on the seat facing sideways so we can all see him. He's got his earphones on. His music is loud enough that even we can hear it. Sort of, at least. It's loud to him, you can count on that. And he's really enjoying it. Look—he's sort of bopping to it. Lucky there's no one sitting next to him. His body wants to dance, and he's almost letting himself do it. He's gawky and awkward. Probably a terrible dancer! But he can't help it, he's drawn to the rhythm. Now he's tilted his head back a bit. He's sort of keeping the beat with his head. He's trying to make it look like his head's just rocking with the rhythm of the moving bus, but he's not fooling anyone. He's mouthing the words! Just a bit . . . but consistently . . . He's starting to do it more . . . Is he going to sing along with the chorus? He might not even realize he's doing it . . . He's closed his eyes! He's revelling in it! He's just decided what his new Favourite Song in the World is . . . those lips keep going . . . oh please . . .

". . . holdin' me now? Nooow-wow-wow-wow-!"

Did you hear that?? His taste in music couldn't possibly be worse! He even did the "now-wow" thing! Everyone looked, too! Those private school girls are clearly snickering. The poker-faced old guy's trying not to laugh. And look at our little rock star—his eyes are still closed. He's completely in his own world.

Does he know what a figure of fun he is for all of us? NOT A CLUE. He's truly un-self-conscious. And what a good time he's having . . .

But Picture It This Way

Now, picture it this way. He's sitting on that bus, but he's not alone. Sitting with him is an attractive woman. She's reading a newspaper, so it's quite acceptable that he would be listening to a walkman. The woman notices everyone looking at them and she watches him for a full minute. She's getting more and more embarrassed, but what's this? She's angry!

She's shaking him by the shoulder. He opens his eyes, and removes his earphones looking worried. Now she's talking to him, her voice starts low, but gets louder. Everyone can hear what she's saying. She's shouting about how ashamed she is to be seen with him. Oh no! She's making points with her rolled up newspaper, whacking him on the nose! The other people on the bus are shifting uncomfortably now. This is so humiliating!

"I hate you! You're so utterly pathetic! I can't pretend that I can fix you anymore! You *disgust* me!"

He's trying to put the earphones back on, but she's grabbed them and thrown his whole tape player out of the window! He's staring at her, and what's this? He's obviously in his thirties but he's starting to cry!

Now does he know what a figure of fun he is for all of us? HE CERTAINLY DOES. He's truly self-conscious. And what a bad time he's having, and will have, every time he listens to music, or even thinks about listening to music. And every time he rides a bus—alone now, of course.

?

France

One of the highest compliments in France is to say that someone has a certain *"je ne sais quoi."* And what does it mean?

I don't know.

I don't speak French. But does the fact that I don't know what it means stop me from enjoying the compliment?

No it doesn't.

In fact, on hearing the phrase, my ignorance allows me to assume any number of compliments, and I can pick and choose which one I want at that time, depending on my mood. Imagine trying to do that with a language you understand!

Old Ladies

We've all experienced the phenomena at some point in our lives of watching a group of old ladies enjoying the company of a Frenchman. Remember how utterly delighted the old ladies always are when the Frenchman says anything that they don't understand. They giggle with glee and imagine what he could mean; each of them trying out the new, unfamiliar, previously *unknown* words.

Compare that to a similar conversation in English.
"Excuse me, do you have any matches?"
"Oooooooh, 'matches'!!! What a lovely word! MA!!!!!!! CCCHHHHHA!!!!!!! ZZZZZZZZZZ!!!!"

The person asking for the matches would at best be confused by what you were doing and sometimes would actually get angry with me.

The behaviour is only acceptable with a language that you *don't know*.

Not Just Our Ignorance

But the sheer joy of a conversation with a foreign person doesn't just come from *our* ignorance of *their* language. Let's not forget *their* ignorance of *ours*. A foreign speaker's difficulty with finding the right English words, or just an incomprehensible accent, is a sure way to turn any conversation into a delightful activity for everyone involved; one part charades, one part comedy routine. And the foreign person invariably derives as much if not more joy from the laughter they're inducing in those around them.

«Where is mah 'otel?»
Hilarious!!!!

«Ah need to buy some cucum*bairz*»
Those crazy Frenchmen!!!

«'Elp, mah wife is needing a doct*eur*!»
Stop it! You're killing me!

Crazy Antics

The connection between being ignorant and giving joy has been recognized and utilized for centuries by entertainers and comedians. We all enjoy watching wacky neighbours in sitcoms, and laughing at their antics. And the people who play those wacky neighbours enjoy making us laugh as much as we enjoy laughing at them.

Even more so than in movies, in real life we love watching people fall over because they *didn't know* there was a banana peel there. Or reading sincere love letters by people who *don't know* how to spell:

"My SOLE cries out for more than you can give."
Is she talking about her foot or her pet fish?
And this one's sweet, but distracting. *"I can't BEER the RESPONSIBITY of mending you."*
This is my favourite.

"I thought there was more to you than this. If I could do it again, I'd spare myself the PANE of wasting time on you, but how could I have known? I thought you were just putting on an act or something. But it's real. Oh, you poor, pathetic man."

Apparently she didn't want to give herself any windows! (Sparing herself the PANE, a pane being a term for a sheet of glass, hence window. Ha ha! I ran through a window once.)

Dog

Consider a dog. Good.

Have you ever been playing a game of fetch-the-stick-and-bring-it-back with a dog and at one point tricked the dog by pretending to throw the stick but actually hiding it behind your back? The dog then tries to find the stick but can't, and runs back with that confused look on its face.

Isn't that look adorable?
Yes it is.

But imagine if the dog, instead of running after the stick, just sat there looking at you, shaking its head and sighing at how stupid the game was, somehow showing in a world-weary shrug just how disgusted he was at your feeble attempt to trick him. The look on his face would be no more adorable than the look you get when you try to play this game with a human.

A huge difference, brought about only by a lack of ignorance.

?

When You Don't Know Someone

When you don't know a person, that in itself is the defining aspect of your relations to each other. And is that a bad thing? Well read the following and then you tell me. Keep in mind, I can't hear you.

Let's say two people were having a drink somewhere. Perhaps one of them had just given a performance of some kind—a lecture, or a demonstration of a philosophy. Maybe the other one had been in the audience and had come up and introduced herself afterwards.

Now here's an important thing to consider: these two people know almost nothing about each other. At this point, anything could happen. Anything! Isn't that exciting? You bet it is! Their relationship hasn't been defined. They're *not sure* if they'll get along. They *don't know* each other's habits—favourite foods, pet-peeves, how they like to spend their time, what joke told to them will make them laugh so hard they'll spit their drink out their noses. They don't know any of those things.

Now take a gander at that look in their eyes. Look at it! They're nervous and uncertain. There's a boundless potential between them. It's possible (and entirely likely) they'll have little or nothing to say. But there's always the chance they'll become everything to each other, the lover and friend that each has always yearned for.

Even Greater Potential

The possibilities are even greater with people you don't know at all. You know the feeling of walking down a sidewalk, or sitting in a crowded theatre, and stealing glances at everyone else. You don't know them. They don't know you. Maybe you'd get along famously. Maybe you'd be friends with them for the rest of your life. Maybe they'd hate you. Maybe they'd like you at first, and then grow fonder of you, but then after a while start criticizing everything you do, the way you think, your pattern of thought, your dog, even questioning your relationship with your own memories, saying things like *"How can you not know?! Your mother quite obviously had you put in an asylum! She just told you it was a university!"*—and then eventually leave in fury, telling you everything that's wrong with you, whacking you over the nose, leaving you a shattered wreck, resenting them for all the nasty things they said but still inexplicably missing them and wishing they'd come back and give you another chance, just another chance, is that so much to ask?

Maybe they'll do all that.

But you *don't know* . . .

What Would Have Happened If He'd Chosen Ignorance

It is often said that mistakes are the greatest teachers. Does it not, then, follow naturally that the mistaken are the second greatest teachers? Yes it does, and yes they are. Even if they (the people who made the mistakes) themselves do not realize it. They are ignorant of their function as examples. They're true inadvertent Ignorami.

With the benefit of hindsight we can dissect the paths we, and others, have chosen and retrace our, or their, steps and try alternate routes, much like someone cheating while reading a Choose Your Own Adventure novel.

Example One:

A young man, Charles Dunworth by name, of St. Cloud, Minnesota, found himself at a point of particular financial distress. He'd been laid off from his job at a soft drink factory for having lipped off his supervisor in a particularly heated exchange. His girlfriend was pregnant with triplets. And he was five payments behind on the car which he'd just driven into a deep muddy ditch while sleeping at the wheel.

He sat on the edge of the sidewalk, sobbing and picking up discarded cigarette butts when the idea came to him that he could multiply what little money he had by betting it on a horse. Furthermore he could increase his earnings tenfold by betting money he didn't have—money he'd acquired in some way other than by gathering it up out of his pockets. Namely, by borrowing it.

Intelligent

Charles was intelligent. He knew that if he were to maximize his chances he'd have to know everything there is to know about horse racing. He soon applied himself like a PhD student, combing through old racing forms, making extensive charts of horse's and jockey's records, trainers' tips, and past bookmakers' odds.

After seven weeks he narrowed his choice down to "Lover's Hands"— a three-year-old gelding his studies showed to be unjustly neglected. He borrowed ten thousand dollars from a local character named "Louie the Lips." He laid it all on his horse to win—every penny of it. The odds against the horse were eighty-eight to one. If his gamble proved correct, he stood to win untold thousands.

The Race

Charles stood in the grandstand as the trumpet call announced the imminent start of the race. He held a set of binoculars up to his eyes, which allowed him to see the gate fly open, the nine horses charge forth, and Lover's Hands immediately trip over a thick wire and break two of its legs as it went into a prolonged roll, whinnying in agony and crushing its jockey. Lover's Hands was promptly shot and boiled into glue.

Oops

Charles now owed Louie the Lips eighteen thousand dollars. He packed a single bag that night and left town, never to be seen again, anonymity being the only safeguard he could trust. He now lives in East Lansing, Michigan. He's changed his name to Charles Wiggins. He works the graveyard shift at the Sunoco station on State St.

Abject Misery

Charles' life is one of abject misery now. It's quite certain he looks back on the series of decisions that brought him to where he is now and wishes he'd chosen differently. Given that neither you nor I are him (unless you are him), we have the luxury to survey his unfortunate, twisted path and ask "Well, What Would Have Happened If He'd Chosen Ignorance?" or—in acronymic form—"WWWHHIHCI?"

"WWWHHIHCI" indeed. What would have. Happened.

Applying a generous slather of ignorance to this man's life would greatly improve it. Let's take a look at how.

WWWHHIHCI

Going back to the start, he wouldn't have lost his job. In the heat of disagreement, his inadequate command of language, combined with a distinct inability to marshal his own thoughts would have left him gape-mouthed and stuttering, absolutely bested by his supervisor. His co-workers would have enjoyed a hearty laugh at his expense, and his supervisor would have felt too good about himself to let such a dependable punching bag go any time soon. It would certainly have guaranteed his job security.

Still gainfully employed he would have been drawing a dependable income as his girlfriend gestated the single fetus he had implanted within her. He wouldn't have known how to have triplets.

He wouldn't have been in arrears with his car payments because he wouldn't have been able to drive one in the first place. Even if he had purchased a car, not being able to drive it, the money he'd have saved on gas he couldn't buy, repairs he didn't have to spring for, parking meters left unfed, and speeding tickets never written to him would pay for the car three times over.

He wouldn't have had the idea pop into his head to increase his money by gambling. It simply wouldn't have occurred to him. Nothing would have.

Supposing betting on a horse had been suggested to him, he wouldn't have studied racing statistics and "information." He would have relied on gut instinct, a stranger's tip or the likeability of a particular horse's name.

He wouldn't have thought to borrow money from an underworld figure, much less known how to get in touch with one. And even if he had, no gangster, upon meeting him, would stoop so low as to take advantage of someone who didn't know what they were getting into.

Supposing he'd found ten thousand dollars, and had presented it in a leather satchel to the betting window clerk he would have stood there and stared at him. The clerk would finally have said "Well?" "Well what." "Which horse do you want to bet this on?" "I don't know" "Well which one do you think will win?" "I have no idea!" and Charles would then have run off. And if we look at racing records from St. Cloud, Minnesota, "I Have No Idea" was a two-year-old stallion who indeed won the very race in which Lover's Hands tripped and died. Given that Charles would have run off without taking his money, it would have been placed on the winning horse, and the money would then be available for him to claim at any time if he ever figured out he'd won it.

Plain

It's plain to see that if he'd chosen ignorance at any point in the preceding series of steps, Louie the Lips would have been paid back in full, Charles would have money to spare and could then finish paying off the car he couldn't drive to work at the soft drink factory doing the job he still had in order to continue earning money to support his soon to be born single fetus. Now who wouldn't envy such a life?

Chapter 5
Know Your Limits And Ignore What You Know

Often, After

Often, after my seminars, people will approach me and tell me how brave I must be. Almost half of the people who do this, it turns out, are referring to my ability to speak in front of the enormous crowds that attend my talks.

"I could never do that," they say, "not in a million years! I get nervous talking to just one person, let alone twelve!"

If I probe deeper, I'll usually find that these people have never actually tried any public speaking at all, and yet they appear so confident in their knowledge that it's something they could never do.

A Similar Reaction

I've noticed a similar reaction to sudden arithmetic. How often have you heard someone, when faced with a simple mathematical task like sharing a restaurant bill, immediately throw up their hands and say "I can't do math!"

Even without looking at the problem, they seem to *know* that they don't have the mathematical know-how to pull it off. The more you try to show them the piece of paper and convince them that they *can* do it, the angrier they'll get.

"Leave me alone!" they'll cry, "I'm telling the manager that you're insane, and you'll be out of a job, buddy!"

Very Fortunate

I feel very fortunate when I deal with these people, because thanks to the excellent parenting I received, I've always known that if *I* can do something, it can't really be that difficult. So obviously, public speaking, philosophy-inventing, and quickly multiplying two seven-digit numbers in your head must be very easy to do.

Constantly Changing

As human beings, we are constantly changing, acquiring new abilities and talents without even knowing it. But most of us never tap into this talent-pool because while what we are capable of is constantly changing, what doesn't change is what we *know* we're capable of.

We must constantly forget ourselves if we are to reach our fullest potentials. The world around us and our own bodies will always keep us from going beyond our abilities, so why use our minds for that? Why bother remembering everything that you can't do, when by forgetting, you might surprise yourself!

If you do that, you never know what a given situation's going to bring out of you. You might find yourself saying:

"Hey, I never knew I could escape from a straitjacket!"
"Hey, I never knew I could pick a lock!"
"Hey, I never knew I could cling to the bottom of a moving vehicle for two hours!"

...or any of dozens of other bits of sudden self-revelation. Who knows what skills you'll pull out of yourself when the situation backs you into a corner and demands it? How exciting!

Do people who know themselves have that experience?
NEVER.

Dramatic Example

One of the most dramatic examples of this phenomenon took place in May 1997 in Charleston, South Carolina.

A local woman, Florence Stephens, was walking to work one morning when she witnessed a car spin out of control as it was catapulted from a collapsing bridge, turning over and over. When the car finally came to rest on the sidewalk, a small boy was pinned underneath the roof. What happened next could have come straight out of a comic book. Mrs. Stephens ran over, dropped her bag, and *lifted the car twelve inches off the ground.* Obviously it wouldn't be a very exciting comic book, but it's remarkable for real life. In any case, it was enough to allow onlookers to pull the little boy out from under the car and get him to an ambulance.

How?

How was this woman capable of such an incredible feat of strength? Perhaps a clue can be found in a statement she made in an interview given to a local reporter who called her later that day at the steroid factory where she worked as a tester.

"My attention was drawn when I heard the bridge snap. I ran over and saw the car pin the little boy. I didn't think about it, I just got my hands under that there car and heaved."

Let's take a closer look at what she said: "was pinned . . . I didn't think about it . . . I just."

Now let's look even closer. In the middle of that sentence you'll find the words: "*I just didn't think about it.*"

Urban Myth

This kind of incident has happened so often now that it has attained the status of urban myth—the passer-by seeing the accident and then exhibiting what appears to be super-human strength to save a little boy. Jack Kirby, the creator of *The Incredibly Hulk* TV show, even cites it as the inspiration for the character he played in that series. And in nearly every case, the person when interviewed will say that they *just didn't think about it.*

What would have happened if Mrs. Stephens *had* thought about it? She would have said "There's no way that I can lift this here car off this here child, I *know* I'm not strong enough"

And that little boy's situation would be much worse today.

It's pretty obvious to me that it was her ignorance that saved the day.

And well, without *The Incredibly Hulk* TV show, who would remember . . . that guy who played him. Not Bill Bixby, the other one.

?

A Story I Received

Here's a story I received from the daughter of a Mrs. Jean Winslow.

The Story

Mrs. Winslow had been bedridden for over four months with what doctors vaguely described as a bad "heart." They told her that if she kept doing as little as possible there was no reason why she shouldn't live for five, ten, or even twenty more years.

Begrudgingly she spent twenty-two out of every twenty-four hours in bed. The longest journey she undertook was a walk into the yard to listen to the birds singing. Even then she had to lean on her daughter's arm.

Disaster

Then disaster struck. The recently built town bridge collapsed, causing major damage including the destruction of the local telephone switchboard. As the town in which Mrs. Winslow lived—Charleston, SC—housed the largest hospital in the county this was a major concern for patients and their relatives. Mrs. Winslow was one of the few local residents with a telephone, so she became the unofficial information desk for the hospital during the crisis. Patients' families were instructed to call Mrs. Winslow, and she would keep them updated as to the statuses of their loved ones.

Work

She embraced her work, and soon became so involved with helping people that she found herself sitting up in bed taking messages. After a few days her eagerness propelled her to use the dresser in her room as a desk, and soon the significant role she played allowed her to forget her weakness enough that she worked from the study downstairs.

In her daughter's words:

> By helping others who were much worse off than she was, she forgot all about herself; and within a matter of days, she was leading a normal life, going back to bed only for her regular eight hours of sleep each night. Those final two weeks of her life were the happiest I'd ever seen her. Obviously, apart from the terrified, drooling agony of her last half-day.

?

Another Example

We can see another example of the wonderful benefits of not being constrained by one's limits in this letter from a seminar attendee.

The Edge

> A number of years ago I witnessed an incredible sales meeting that changed everything for me. All of the sales staff were called into the meeting room and as we entered we saw the vice-president standing at one end of the room with Doug, a sales representative like myself. Doug looked uncomfortable, but the VP was excited and eager to start the meeting. He opened with a question.
> "What's the average earnings of you sales representatives?"
> We established that it was about $16,000 a year, with one or two reps pushing towards $20,000. Then another question:
> "You want to know what Doug's earnings were? $70,000."
> While we were gasping amazement the VP took a step to one side and nudged Doug forward.
> "Now, I want you all to look very closely at Doug. Look at him! What does Doug have that the rest of you don't have? He earned $70,000, that's four and a half times the average! What's Doug's edge?
> "Is he four and a half times as intelligent as the rest of you? No. I checked his personnel records and he's average—actually a little lower than average.
> "We can see that he's not remotely attractive physically, so that's not it. Is he somehow more charming, does he have a certain 'je-ne-sais-quoi' that makes him an irresistible seller? No. He's kind of annoying—very

annoying in fact, with serious body-odor problems and a habit of stammering. Look at him—he's fidgeting now."

And indeed Doug was fidgeting. And unattractive.

The VP continued.

"Does he work harder than the rest of you? No. We've been keeping close tabs on him since we noticed his success, and actually he's put in less hours than anyone else here, taking time off work to visit a therapist and to sign up with that dating agency. And when he is here he spends a lot more than the average amount of time surfing the internet, trying to find tips on how to have more confidence around other people.

"Was he raised by better parents? No! He wa— Hey! Doug! Where are you going? We haven't found out what your edge is! Get back here ya crybaby! Ahh, nuts. The rest of you, get back to work. GET MORE SALES, YA LOUSY BUMS!"

The meeting ended there. Doug never even came in to pick up his things, but his legacy remained.

Doug's Legacy

I had previously thought that I knew the limits of my job, but now I knew that my *knowledge* was wrong. I knew that there was a way to get more sales, but what?

I spent the next few years trying new ways of selling, searching for that *unknown* edge that Doug had had. I discovered a great deal I never would have if I had *known* Doug's secret. I found my own ways of improving through trial and error. Now, just ten years later, my sales earnings routinely reach $40,000 a year—all through *not knowing*.

I asked the VP about Doug a few years ago and he said "Oh, didn't you hear? It was a typo. The report should have said Doug only made $7,000. That guy was a dud. A real dud."

I'd like to believe that there's something more, though. I've seen Doug once or twice since then. I've tried to ask him about his edge but he always just packs up his things and walks away. I notice that his hat has more money in it than the other panhandlers' hats. Four and a half times more, I'd say!

?

The Last Story In This Chapter

Here's another very moving story that was left on my answering machine.

> Yeah, hi. I think this is the right number, there wasn't a name on the out-going message, but I think I recognized your voice. That's a funny message—really sounded like you don't have a clue how these machines work.
>
> Anyway, I couldn't wait to tell you about what happened after I began to put the Power of Ignorance into practice.
>
> I run a very small engineering firm. We're usually not big enough to get the big contracts, and have to live on the hand-me-downs of bigger firms. It's soul-destroying work. The company's not doing very well, and I was seriously considering giving it all up.
>
> Before I attended your seminar I always *knew* that there were very real limits on what we could do, and I never even bid on the bigger contracts, the kind I *knew* I could never win, and I *knew* that even if I did win them, I wouldn't be able to build the thing!
>
> So when the opportunity to submit a bid on a major town project came in, my initial reaction was to say "No, it's too big a job, I only have two engineers in the company (including me) and neither of us has ever designed anything but a short stretch of sidewalk before. Heck, Russell, (the other engineer) is usually drunk by noon! I *know* I shouldn't bid on this thing,

I wouldn't get it, and if I did, it could be the worst thing that's ever happened to me."

Remembered

Hi, it's me again. The machine beeped and I wasn't done.

So lemme see . . . small company . . . contract came in . . . wasn't gonna bid on it . . . oh yeah! But then I remembered some of your words from the seminar. You said, " . . . "

You know what? I don't remember what you said now, but I remember it really inspired me. Something about a dog, I think, walking on its hind legs. Or was it? It doesn't matter, but dammit, this is going to bother me all day now. Oh, what was it you said? (sigh) Anyway, the point is, I decided that I didn't *know* that I *wouldn't* get the contract, so I put in a bid.

We won. We're still in the design phase now, and that's exciting, new and *unknown* territory. Thanks to you and your seminar, not only has my company turned around, I've also re-discovered the joy of solving big problems. I feel like an engineer again, thanks to the Power of Ignorance.

That's it! You said, "If you don't know that it isn't possible, then, good for you!" Was that you? Or was it that other guy? Were you the one with the shirt? To be honest, I went to so many seminars that day, I was that desperate, and you're all a big blur now. You were definitely the funniest one though.

Beep!

Me again. Man, your machine is a Nazi!

Anyway I just wanted to say thanks for the much needed inspiration. The plans for the bridge are looking great.

Hey, how about when it's done you come on down here to Charleston and we'll drive across it together.

Aw, Shucks

As we can see, this engineer found new hope, new financial success, and even a renewed sense of purpose from applying *my* principle, "You don't know what isn't possible, therefore anything isn't possible."

See?

Lion

Here's another example, perhaps more useful in your everyday lives, of the amazing benefits of ignorance. Shortly before I left home my parents and I visited a safari park. As they had learned from reading scientific journals, the most important thing a child needs growing up is plenty of water, so they had been encouraging me to drink as much as I could on the way there. We were driving very slowly through the park when it became clear to me that I would have to answer, let's say, "the call of the wild."

Safe Side

My parents very carefully made sure that we were on the safe side of the high fences which separated the vicious zebras from the rest of the animals. Then they stopped the car.

"Don't forget your lucky steak!" they called after me as I walked to some bushes.

"I have it!" I replied, indicating the pound of raw meat, given to me as a gift just that morning, which was hanging from a string around my neck. After I finished what I was doing I went back to the car, but found nothing but empty road. I realized I had somehow got lost, and my parents must be waiting for me in a spot that looked exactly like the one where I was standing, except with a car where these tire tracks were. I was sure they must be very worried.

Searching

I spent some time searching for the car, but with no luck. As it was getting dark I decided to try and find the way out on my own.

This was not as simple a task as it might seem, because I had to do this while at the same time avoiding all the other cars I saw. (My parents had been very careful to warn me that safari parks often contained cars full of dangerous child-catchers, who would kidnap any little boy they saw and make him work forever in the dreaded peach-mines.)

Avoid The Zebras

I soon came upon the high fence which meant the edge of the dangerous zebra enclosure. I decided to follow the fence and go around the zebras entirely.

After about an hour of walking I realized I was being followed. I turned and saw a whole family of lions!!! There were three adults and several cubs. The adults were advancing very slowly towards me, and I knew I was in terrible danger. It was only my parents' graphic descriptions of people being slowly and agonizingly killed by zebras that saved me from entirely giving in to panic and climbing the fence. That would have been jumping from the frying pan and into the fire! I knew from my own reading that lions were dangerous, but I also knew that they couldn't be anywhere near as dangerous as the vicious beasts in that enclosure. (Apparently "zebra" is actually a Swahili word meaning, "the stripy devil who kills slowly, especially little boys with big brains.")

My parents had very thoughtfully prepared me for meeting lions, but in my terror I couldn't remember what they'd told me to do. I believe now that it was my ignorance of that advice that saved my life.

Worked It Out Myself

You see, faced with survival from lions, and unable to remember the proper procedures, I had to come up with my own solution to the problem.

One of my only friends at that time was a boy called Leo. I knew that Leo actually meant "lion," so in my childish naiveté I decided that I would treat the three advancing lions as if they were three "Leo's."

What Doesn't Leo Like?

First of all, I remembered that Leo hated to run fast, so I sprinted away. When I was too exhausted to go any further I looked back and saw that one lion had indeed stopped following me.

Then I remembered that Leo was a vegetarian. Reluctantly, and with a silent promise to my parents that I would do whatever it took to make them forgive me, I took off my lucky steak, one of the few gifts they had ever given me, and threw it hard at the lions. One of them grabbed it, and ran away, presumably to bury the foul meat-smell far away from its delicate lion nose.

The final lion was getting very close now, and that was when I remembered that my friend Leo hated to be beaten up with a big stick. I grabbed a branch from a nearby tree and swung it with all my might at the lion. After a minute or so this final lion left me alone too.

I Had Survived

As I watched it run off back to its family I became very conscious of the fact that I had survived. I hadn't had access to the knowledge of how to deal with lions and my reasoning had been illogical and utterly flawed, but somehow I had come up with a way to save myself from not just one, but three full-grown lions.

I kept walking for a whole day, following the fence, trying to skirt around the zebra enclosure, but I still didn't reach the end. Finally, emboldened by my encounter with the three Leos, I decided to brave the zebras.

I concentrated very hard on the weaknesses of my friend Dudley, who always wore a stripy sweater, and once again my ignorant approach worked. The many zebras I saw were easily dissuaded from hurting me by my threat to tell their parents that I'd seen them cheating on their homework, and eventually I found my way, still avoiding the childcatchers, to the administration building.

A Tearful Reunion

The police came to re-unite me with my family, but I was obviously in shock, as even though I was 100 percent certain that I was giving them my correct address, the one that it had been drilled into me to repeat if ever I got lost, the address was completely wrong. There was no house there at all!

Eventually they were able to trace my parents using the vehicle registration of which the safari administration had a record and I was taken home. Mummy and Daddy were trying to ease their worry for me by drinking champagne, and they had invited all their friends over who were trying to cheer them up with festive hats, dancing and a big banner saying, "Gone at last!."

I could tell they were very disappointed that I had forgotten their advice as well as at the loss of my lucky steak.

Lucky

Later on, I remembered the advice they had given me on dealing with lions, and realized how lucky I was to be alive, because my methods had been completely wrong.

Lion experts at that time held that the safest response was to approach the lion slowly, with your hands stretched behind your back and your head tilted back. I never did see the copy of "Lions Weekly" from which my parents had obtained this information, but just a few years later I found out that scientists had rethought this and found that running away, throwing meat and hitting them with a stick were actually very good ways to survive a lion encounter.

Who Knows?

Who knows what other problems can be solved just by forgetting one's parents advice?

Maybe there's a better way to put out a fire than by throwing your own gasoline-soaked body onto the flames, or a friendlier greeting to a policeman than playfully grabbing his gun.

Who knows, indeed?

Chapter 6
From Ignorance Comes Confidence

Human Interaction

Human society is an incredibly complicated system. Every day each of us will interact with anywhere from a few dozen to a few hundred other humans, and every single one of these interactions will have some effect on our lives. Sometimes that effect will be obvious and instantaneous, other times not. Sometimes it will be larger than others, sometimes smaller, but the constant is that each interaction will definitely affect us.

I Live Alone

Now, I realize some of you are probably saying "Hey! This book's no good for me! I live alone! Stranded on a desert island! My life is never affected by interactions with human beings! I don't talk much any more! AAaaaah! Footprints?"

And to you, I say yes, you're right, this section doesn't apply to you at all, and while obviously you do have plenty of time on your hands, you might want to use it building a shelter or doing something more useful and wait for my follow up book, *The Power Of Ignorance For People Stranded Alone On A Desert Island.*

The Rest Of Us

For the rest of us, interactions with people other than ourselves do have a huge influence on our well-being.

Job interviews, business negotiations, first dates, criminal trials, going to the doctor, getting on a bus, asking a lifeguard for assistance, pointing out to a parent that your hand is trapped in a door, and meeting a group of five influential people for the first time are just three kinds of interactions that we all experience in our daily lives, and how successful those interactions are for us can change our level of professional success, our financial well-being, our children's futures, our emotional state, our pancreases, our ability to ride a bus, our enjoyment of a trip to the beach, our ability to hold things, and our direction in life.

One Way To Push

There are many ways that we can increase the level of success of each interaction, but one way to push any interaction towards a favourable outcome is to approach it with confidence.

Think about it:

The interviewer is going to give the job to the applicant who seems confident that they're exactly the right person for it.

Your opposite number in a business negotiation will walk all over you if you don't seem confident of your position.

And you're a lot more likely to be stuck in a painful, hideous relationship if you're too frightened, or don't have the *confidence*, to politely bring up just one or two tiny things that have been bothering you.

Where Does Confidence Come From?

And where does confidence come from?
Why do some people have it and others don't?
How can you get more confidence?

The answers to those three questions are, in no particular order:

Because they have more Ignorance.
By tapping into *your* Power of Ignorance.
From Ignorance.

Often when people are performing a task and lose confidence, the reason behind it will be that they became *self-conscious*. i.e. *aware* of them*selves*. So it stands to reason that confidence would come from being self-*un*conscious—the confidence only sleeping people really achieve.

The Confidence Of The Asleep

How often have you looked at someone who obviously worries less than you about their appearance and what other people think and said to yourself "I could never pull that off! I wish I had their confidence!"

Well, you do have that confidence, and more. For eleven hours every night.

Right now you're probably saying "What?! What the deuce?! Vaugen, this is too much! I have put up with your nonsense for long enough! With your insane ramblings! Ignorance!? Poppycock! Bladderdash! Fiddlesticks! Applesauce, sir. I say to you . . . Apple. *Sauce*. Now, what's this about me pulling off confidence eleven hours every night. I demand an explanation! This instant! Harrumph!"

Well, OK.

Let's take a look at you at your most confident, and see if you don't agree with me once I'm done.

"Very well sir, but remember, you're on thin ice, sonny-me-lad. Very. Thin. *Ice*."

Your Face

There you are. Your face is a picture of serenity. You're obviously not worried about other people's opinions. You're relaxed enough that you don't mind that your hair is a swirling mess, and you haven't bothered to shave or put on make-up. You're happy, and you're happy to show that you're happy, smiling to yourself, even laughing! If you talk at all you're not concerned with making sense. But hey! You've stopped talking! Listen to that! Now you're making an impossibly loud sawing noise with every outhalation! And you're drooling, there's a puddle of it on the pillow. And your breath stinks and you don't care.

And how, you might wonder, have you achieved this picture of perfect confidence?

I'm sure the answer will astound you.

Ready?

You're *asleep*.

"What? Asleep? That was utterly unexpected, and yet it makes ... complete ... sense. I've ... wronged you. No, I have. I'm a proud man, but let no one say that I don't admit when I'm wrong. I've impugned you my boy, and made a veritable ass of myself in the process. I don't know what they'll say at the club. I am heartily sorry. Would you do me the honour of shaking my hand and granting me your forgiveness?"

As astonishing as it may sound, once you think about it you'll see that it actually does make complete sense. You do have this confidence within you, and let it come out every time you go to sleep.

This Confidence In Waking Life

Imagine if you could bring the confidence of the asleep into your waking life.

Think about it. Picture a high-powered executive walking into a board meeting. But he's not wearing an expensive suit and a well-groomed mask of confidence. He doesn't need to. He has *real* confidence. After all he's only wearing his underwear. He's kicking randomly and stealing all the blankets from the other executives. And not apologizing for it either! He doesn't care about his appearance at all. See, he's not sucking in his gut, and he's paying no attention to his erect penis. If only the other executives could do the same. And all this confident behaviour isn't done for show, with hesitation, or with skittish glances to each side.

And you know what? I don't think anyone's going to be disagreeing with him today!

?

Train Station

I'd like you to imagine you are in a train station full of people. The various paths people take intersect as they walk from one point in the station to another. Now imagine that *you* have to walk through.

You want to get through as quickly as possible, but you don't want to walk into anyone. Inevitably there will be many times when your path crosses another person's, and the two of you will have to decide who will go first. If you're more confident you'll take the lead, but if you're less confident you'll let them go first or change direction entirely. If both of you have little confidence you may well find yourself doing an awkward dance, each trying so hard to get out of the other's way that you might end up bumping into each other after all!

The more confidently you walk through that station, the more likely the other people are to walk around you without you changing direction at all, and the faster you'll reach your destination.

"But What Does This Have To Do With Ignorance?" You May Ask.

"But what does this have to do with ignorance?" you might ask.

Well, in 1981 this exact scenario was recreated for an experiment at Brunel University in London, England which provides powerful insight into the link between confidence and ignorance.

The students at the Robotics Enthusiasts Society each designed a robot that would be able to pass from one end of a crowded train station to the other. The robots would be judged on their speed and on their ability to avoid collisions.

The university obtained access to London's Waterloo Station from 2:00 a.m. until 7:00 a.m. one morning; volunteer students were assigned routes a-zigging and a-zagging the room, simulating commuters.

The robots were found to behave in ways similar to humans. Most manoeuvred their way through the crowd maintaining an average speed a little slower than walking, thanks to occasional tangles with students. A few robots failed to make it across at all, getting stuck in corners and cafes. One got so lost it wasn't found until the next morning, on the railway tracks halfway to Brighton! All of them took much longer to cross the concourse than a human, with an average of five collisions each.

One Robot

But one robot literally stood out from the crowd. It passed through the room in less than one tenth of the time taken by the next fastest robot, and it only bumped into one student. It crossed 340 metres in just over fifteen seconds. That's an average speed of fifty miles per hour!

What was the difference between this robot and the others? Was it better designed? Had it been somehow programmed to detect people in a fifty-metre radius and so avoid them far better than its fellows? No. Quite the opposite, in fact. Its processor had been damaged and it didn't recognize any obstacles, and *ignored* them. It didn't waste time thinking about anything, and instead of the robot getting out of people's way, the people got out of *its* way.

Proof

It was never their intention, but the Brunel RES's experiment had proven that the chief component in confidence is ignorance.

Ironically enough, *they don't even know they've proved this*.

Their published findings—the only university paper I've ever seen called an "inquest"—make no reference to this discovery at all, preferring to dwell more on the "death of a student by mechanical trampling" aspects of the event. They've completely ignored that they witnessed the birth of A.I.: Artificial Ignorance.

?

Dancing

Imagine for a moment that you are watching a roomful of people dancing, perhaps you're at a disco, or a nightclub, or the insect house of a zoo.

Watch the movements of the people on that dance floor. Watch their bodies. Look closely at their faces.

If you split the dancers into two groups you will see that there are those who dance confidently and those who don't.

Most of the people who aren't confident will be concentrating very hard on what they're doing, stomping their heavy feet to a rhythm that only occasionally coincides with that audible to human beings. Often these people will only be dancing to make their dance-partners happy, and every second on that dance floor causes them intense emotional pain. They have no confidence, *because they don't know how to dance.*

Those People

Now look at those people who do have confidence. A small amount of them will be very good dancers, they'll probably look very serious, concentrating very hard on executing difficult and often dangerous manoeuvres, the result of years of dance training. These people are dancing confidently *because they do know how to dance.*

But far more of the confident dancers will fit into another category. They'll be smiling, or laughing. They'll not necessarily be sticking to the rhythm, but they will be enjoying themselves, perhaps playing a game at doing a cheesy mock-tango. Yes, these people don't know how to dance, but they are dancing confidently because they **don't know** that **they don't know** *how to dance.*

The Point I'm Labouring To Make

Being good at a required skill is certainly one way to get more confidence, but being good at something will rarely get you as much confidence as just *not knowing you're bad at it.*

I'm sure we've all at one time experienced a long-winded, pointless, unamusing yet confidently told anecdote whose utter failure to get a response never stops the teller from launching into another one. Or worse, the same one again.

And who hasn't read a book written by some hack with no idea how repetitive, self-contradictory and just plain stupid their writing is?

And I bet there's no one among us who has not been bombarded with advice from someone inexplicably oblivious to the fact that their counsel inevitably leads to failure, occasionally even tragedy and disaster.

And Another Thing

I don't want to say that you shouldn't have any skills at all. It's OK if you really can do something well. For instance I am actually a wonderful dancer, combining grace with the sensual heat and soft step of a particularly agile cat.

But you'll never be able to learn every skill required in every interaction. However, the not-knowing-you're-bad approach is something that gets easier and easier the more you do it. In fact after you've been using it for some time you'll find yourself not knowing you're bad at things you've never even heard of!

?

Don't Think At All

As we've seen elsewhere in this book, too much knowledge of our lack of ability is one way that our minds can short-circuit our confidence. But it's not the only way. Any thinking at all will prevent us from behaving confidently.

This point is very well illustrated by the following story told to me by a man who'd attended one of my seminars in Muncie, Indiana.

> I was on a management training weekend in Northern Maine. The company had assembled a group of thirteen executives from across the country whose results were not quite up to par. They gathered us together and sent us on a two-day hike into the mountains.
>
> It was mid-way through the first day when we realized none of us had brought food, maps, compasses, or changes of clothing. We were all in upper management and had assumed some subordinate would take care of all that!
>
> Of course our first reaction was terror. What

would we eat? Things went from bad to worse an hour later when we found we were also hopelessly lost. We didn't know how long it would take to find our way back, or what we'd wear when our clothes got soiled, which had already happened to a few of us (not me though). Soon we were all panicking. Arguments broke out. Accusations flew. I could tell some people were already thinking about who they would eat first.

My Knowledge

But I remembered my boy-scout training. This was my big chance! They would see that with my knowledge I could lead them. We'd all be united and I'd bring them home to safety.

I stepped forward.

"Excuse me everyone! Um, may I have your attention please? Hello? Yes, sorry. But uh . . ."

They were all looking at me. Between the bored, annoyed expressions I could see the hope in some of their faces.

"I was a . . . boy-scout. Long time ago now . . . I don't want to say how long . . . Let's just say, um, disco was big!"

There was a single cough. And I could hear crickets.

"It was the seventies."

"Get on with it!"

"Sorry . . . um . . . I think moss grows on the uh . . . uh . . . uh . . . Never Eat Shredded . . . was it Wheat or Wieners? Anyway. We can find our way back because . . ."

Interrupted

"Hey Fellas!" said a clear virile voice, "Don't listen to that egg-head!"

It was Skip McGraw—a man I'd met the day

we'd arrived. He was the kind of guy people took to immediately. He was tall, good-looking and well-built. I didn't know why *he'd* been sent on this course. He must have been great at managing his thousands of underlings! I'd liked him since our first meeting when I'd helped him figure out the latch on the outhouse door.

"Follow me everyone!" he said, stomping off with long confident strides of his magnificent legs.

Instantly everyone followed the path he'd started blazing through the dense underbrush with his barrel chest and capable arms.

"Wait!" I said, raising my voice, "um . . . I really think I'll be able to get us out of here."

Embarrassed

But my twelve companions were long gone. I was too embarrassed to try to catch up with them, or to check in at the lodge when I found my way back. I just got in my car and went home.

So ashamed was I that I couldn't show my face at work. When, after two weeks, my company hadn't even phoned to find out why I'd stopped coming in I realized I'd truly blown my big chance.

I moved on with my life, but I never forgot that important lesson: in leadership, confidence and thinking don't mix.

What This Means

I don't know what lesson one could draw from that man's experience, but maybe it's this one: in terms of leadership, thinking doesn't go well with confidence.

If I Knew Then

"If I knew then what I know now, boy, I tellya, that'd certainly be something, it sure would."

The above is a very commonly expressed sentiment. The implication is that we know more now, individually, than we did in the past.

Our experiences stamp certain lessons on us—many of them painful and difficult. If we had some way of travelling back in time and warning ourselves, we could have avoided going through those experiences that made us learn those lessons. Thus we wouldn't have the knowledge gained by those lessons and, by extension, any impulse to travel back in time and warn ourselves. And if this was the case we would have stumbled right on into those situations which ended up teaching us those lessons like we did anyway. And the painful lessons we learned from these experiences would then implant a desire to travel back in time and warn ourselves to avoid those very same situations and thus learn those lessons.

Yes. I'm dizzy too.

But consider the implication in this wish and this whole pattern of thought: that in the past, we were ignorant.

Looking Back

Does anyone look back on themselves and say "You know, when I think about who I was even just a few years ago, and what I did, and all the decisions I made, I just beam with pride. I sure was smart."

No they don't. They shake their heads. They marvel that they're still alive. They laugh wistfully at the young fool they had so recently been.

Five-year-olds look down on two-year-olds. They're such babies, they say. Look at them, playing with their baby toys. Drooling. Wearing diapers. Taking naps. Crying. Pooping their pants. They can't even multiply single digit numbers. They don't know anything.

Eight-year-olds look down on five-year-olds. They're such babies, they say. Look at them, playing with their crayons. Unable to divide fractions or multiply negatives. Wetting the bed. Crying. They're stupid. They don't know anything.

Twelve-year-olds look down on eight-year-olds. Buncha babies. Look at those stupid cartoons they're watching. Those silly toys they play with. How scared they are to cross the street. They have bedtimes. They wear those bright kids clothes. They can't calculate pi to a hundred decimal points or figure out the square root of prime numbers. They don't know anything!

Sixteen-year-olds look down on twelve-year-olds. What a bunch of little kids they are. No body hair. No deodorants. They can't drive, they spell out swear words instead of saying them, they can't get into PG-13 movies, they still have bedtimes. They can't do the simplest manipulations of sines and cosines, much less logs. They think they're all grown up, but they don't know a thing.

Nineteen-year-olds look down on sixteen-year-olds. Look at them—what a bunch of toddlers. They have curfews. They can't vote, can't drink, can't see restricted movies. They've never stayed up all night. And if you asked them to calculate the vector on two moving objects, one overtaking the other at an unspecified rate, considering wind speed and surface friction, would they be able to tell you? Hell, no!! What do they know about anything?

A Pattern

Have you started to notice a pattern? If not, that's okay. The point is that we constantly look down on others of a younger age, and memories of ourselves at those same younger ages, always concluding that when we were whichever age we're talking about, we thought we knew everything when in fact we knew nothing.

Is there ever an age we reach in which we stop saying this? Yes there is. It's the age I'm at right now.

But there's certainly something to be learned from noticing this tendency. Namely that we really don't know anything. Knowledge is an illusion. We, all of us, are in a never-ending process of realizing that the views we had and the estimations we held of our own knowledge and abilities only a short time before were pure twaddle.

Until you reach my age.

Dreams

Look at any advertisement for a self-help book or seminar and you will see claims that this or that system will help you achieve your goals and realize your dreams.

I have personally been an integral part of the fulfillment of many people's ambitions, and it is a wonderful feeling, but we'll deal later on in this book with how I can help *you* in that way.

I'd like to look now at what is perhaps an even more important service that I render.

Recently a man approached me after a seminar and told me

"Last night I won an Oscar and the people cheered for longer than they ever had, and they carried me down the street on their shoulders, and a beautiful woman who I'd never seen spoke to me in Spanish and I don't speak Spanish but I knew what she was saying."

"None of that happened." I replied "That was a dream."

"Oh."

You see, while I have always been proud of the fact that I have helped literally countless people realize their dreams, I am even more proud of those times when I have helped people to realize their dreams *are dreams*.

Chapter 7
Achieve The Possible

Knowing Too Much

A lot of times in our lives, we find ourselves hemmed in, constrained by what we tell ourselves we can't do.

You know what I'm talking about. Those moments when you suddenly find yourself *knowing too much*.

When you catch yourself saying things like:

"I *know* this won't work."

"I *know* they won't accept me."

"I *know* I'm just a fake."

"A big fat fake with a book deal."

"The publishers only agreed to do this book as a tax write-off."

These awkward moments of self-realization can be very damaging indeed. They can undo in seconds the confidence that you have built up through years of good luck, hard work and a pig-headed refusal to see your own shortcomings.

Thanks

But thanks to the Power of Ignorance, there is a method available to you to bat away that awkward self-knowledge.

That method is called the Power of Ignorance Mantra.

By using the 'Igmantra' you too can silence that voice in your head that tells you what you *can't* do.

When one of these crises of confidence occurs, stop and focus.

Focus on what is known as "middle air."

Focus and breathe . . . *without thinking!* (*YOU MAKE MY HIPS BUCK BABY! GIRL THERE AIN'T NO MAYBE! WHAT'S FINE IS FINE, CAN'T GET YOU OFF OF MY MIND!*)

Now that you're enjoying the buoyant sensation of the

"middle air," feel the igmantra seep up through you, naturally releasing. Now relax and say the following word out loud:

"Duh."

This is the Igmantra. Try it again.

"Duh."

Feels good, doesn't it?

"Duh."

Yes it does.

"Duh."

You should be able to feel some of your negative thoughts disappearing. If not, then you're OBVIOUSLY DOING IT WRONG!
I'm sorry.
Try saying it again, louder.

"DUH."

If that's not loud enough, go even louder,

"DUH."

Now lean over a little and say it,

"Duh."

OK. That was good, but you lost the volume,

"Duh."

More.

"*DUH.*"

One more time, loud, leaning and as emphatic as you can . . .

"*DUH!*"

Now pull it back just a little.

"*DUH.*"

Wonderful.

The Igmantra is the most useful item in the Power of Ignorance Toolbox. By focusing on it, you can blot out unwanted knowledge completely.

Use the Igmantra

Use the Igmantra wherever you need it.

Perhaps at work while dealing with a difficult customer. Or later on in a disciplinary meeting with your boss. Or the next day at a very important job interview.

In your personal life, you can use the igmantra while in the middle of a difficult conversation with a significant other with whom you intend to spend the rest of your life.

"I don't want to be with you any more."
"DUH."
"I mean it, I'm calling the police."
"DUH."
"You're coming with us."
"DUH."
"How do you plead?"
"DUH."
"Mr. Vaguen, if you do not answer the next question

appropriately, you will be subject to a psychiatric evaluation."
"DUH."
"You again?"
"DUH."
"You're not getting away this time."
"DUH?"
"I can tell by your self-assured face and how you said that 'duh' as a question that you think you *are* going to get away again, but I can assure you that you're not."
"DUH?"
"Yes, really. You're stuck here, ya nut!"
"DUH?"
"Stop that. You're not gettin' away!"
"DUH?"
"NO."
"DUH?"
"OK, I've had enough, hit him boys!"
BZZZZZT!
"Now whaddya say?"
"... duh"
"What?"
"... duh"
BZZZZZZZZT
"..."
BZZZZZZZZZT
"..."
BZZZZZZZZZZT!!!
"..."
"OK boys, he's had enough, let's get outta here!"
(SLAM!)
"... DUH."

In Public

Most importantly, use the igmantra in public.
Yes, in public.
I know what you're thinking. "But people will stare at me. They'll be confused, man! Like wavy gravy! Like a chocolate

14 STEPS TO USING YOUR IGNORANCE   85

submarine! Like a Ferris wheel for the flies!"

Yes they will.

And what a warm feeling that will give you, to see their confusion, knowing that you have helped them tap into their Power of Ignorance.

Because as we know, confusion is the boulevard to Ignorance.

?

What Do People Really Want?

What is it that human beings thirst for more than anything else? Apart from a glass of water, that is!

Hilarity aside, what about their spiritual needs? What's the *emotional* glass of water they crave?

A great and important eighteenth-century social scientist whose name escapes me at the moment devoted his whole life, sacrificing his wealth, social position and his marriage to work on his magnum opus—a nine-volume text detailing the hundred things human beings need more than any other.

Here they are:

Number One: Ye Feelinge of Being Importante

As children we spend a great deal of our time trying to win the attention of adults. As we grow older, the methods change, but the need does not. Some of us, like the important scientist mentioned above, will spend our entire lives working to ensure that the attention we get continues beyond our deaths.

We needn't worry about the other hundred items on that old guy's list. (Between you and me, they're rarely cited anyway. And quite dull.)

The Difference Between People and Animals

What's the biggest difference between man and the animals? I don't know. Maybe a scientist would. Or a farmer. Or an animal.

But I do know this—people are constantly striving for a feeling of significance in a way that few animals ever do.

And yet, how many people ever achieve importance of any kind? Almost none. What a doomed ambition weighs us all down! What a hellish need we find unconsciously strapped onto our souls—one destined to leave us broken, bitter, and foisting our unfulfilled and unrealistic dreamed up "potential" onto our children. Either that or to resent those children for being happy and carefree, and to do everything we can to crack that happiness of theirs in half and slice it into unrecognizable strips, leaving it to be picked at by the crows.

Animals Again

Now consider the animals once again. Could it be that they don't strive for any greater position in the world . . . because they *don't know* that such a thing exists? The average animal's knowledge is limited to its immediate surroundings. To a chicken its nest is the whole world. Dogs have no cognizance of there being dogs in other countries that they could ever be admired by. Ferns never fret that they won't be remembered by future generations of ferns.

And if you tried to explain these things they'd never understand you, try though they might. Their ignorance reigns triumphant. What a shield against the unhappiness known as "ambition" it is! If we cultivate our ignorance we could all be as happy as the ferns.

You Don't Expect Me

But you don't honestly expect me to erase the knowledge from my own head that there's a whole world outside my door and billions of people out there? And how significant those facts are to someone like me as regards to my previously established need for ye feeling of being important, do you?

Yes I do. That's exactly what I expect. But I'll admit it takes a pretty advanced ignoramus to reach that level. In the meantime here's something anyone can do to shed the yoke of ambition.

Lower Your Standards

Yes, it's that simple. If it's your dream to become an astronaut, let's face it, that just isn't going to happen.

But what if you changed that dream to *wanting to look at a picture of an astronaut*? Easy! You could do it in an afternoon. And think of what a privileged position you'd be in, having not only fulfilled your lifelong dream, but to be able to do it again any time you like. It would be as if King Arthur had found the Holy Grail in his kitchen cupboard and then drank Tang out of it every day. And who doesn't love Tang? No one. Even astronauts drink it.

Smothered

Here are some other toned-down dreams:

- A person who always wanted to be a movie star could change that to having always wanted to watch a movie.
- An aspiring circus performer might instead dream of waving at a person on the sidewalk while riding by in a bus.
- A hopeful football player might lay any hope of playing in the Superbowl aside in order to picture themselves someday pouring a perfect glass of milk.

And think of how satisfying it would be to drink that perfect glass of milk. It would feel even better if that person gave that glass to the calf who would have drank it if its mother hadn't been trapped, domesticated, and put to work. Picture that—a human giving a perfect glass of milk to a calf, both of them unfettered by stupid, impossible dreams—their minds functioning on a single wavelength. What a peaceful, hopeful vision for us all.

Insane People

What makes people go insane? The only people who really know the answer to this are the insane people themselves. Their answers obviously can't be trusted. Scientists tell us fifty per cent of the time it's due to chemical imbalance. But what of the remaining three sixths?

Well, for many of them it's the prolonged and repeated torment of there having been someone who should have loved them but didn't. For others it's the pain of having never gained that feeling of importance.

Loonies

Many loonies create elaborate fantasy lives in which all of their ambitions have been realized. They don't live in the same world you or I do—they inhabit magical lands in which they're kings, or spiritual guides, or university students, and stubbornly refuse to notice the gaps between their version of the world and the *real* world.

Nuts

What's to be done with nuts like these? Nothing. If they were to ever realize their worlds were as insubstantial as a house of cards, everything they knew would topple like a stack of chairs of such different styles as to be well-nigh unstackable (you know the kind I mean!).

Those pitiful crackpots would be broken and possibly lose their minds. They might even take what they could of their old, nice mental landscape and retreat further and further into the odd, pathetic imaginary reality they'd concocted, burrowing deeper into the firmament of their own made-up nonsense, grasping a few initially sound principles and repeating them endlessly, driving them into the ground as they sat there, spinning endless variations on a pretty limited premise.

If only these people had learned what the cows and the ferns and the dogs have to teach us.

?

Dog

Consider a dog.

Now a dog understands certain simple things, like hunger or territory, or "Who's my little snuffly-woo yes you are. Yes you are. Ooooh, wess woo warr!"

But more complex matters like mathematics or boardgames would be ununderstandable to even the smartest *German Shepherd*.

Explaining Monopoly

Try explaining Monopoly to your dog.

(Of course you'd have to imagine you had a lot of free time on your hands!)

(Because you don't go out much, and you just don't know what to do!)

(And you don't have many friends!)

(OK—any friends!)

(Something about you keeps people at a distance and you find it difficult to relate to people!)

(Even the guy from the convenience store has offered to have everything delivered!)

(Just so he doesn't have to talk to you!)

(You spend most of your time sitting around in your underwear!)

Beating Him

No matter how much patience you had with your dog, no matter how great your skills as a teacher, no matter how clear, simple and direct your language, at best that dog would be a mediocre Monopolist. And believe me you'd get pretty tired of beating him nearly three games out of four.

But more importantly, what would he do with this knowledge?

Could he play Monopoly with other dogs when you weren't there?

Would he ever stop trying to build houses on the railroads? Or peeing on Free Parking?

Would he feel more like a "good boy"?

Would he ever choose any Monopoly piece other than the dog? Or occasionally the old boot?

No he doesn't.

Mediocre Monopolists ... In Life!

It makes you think, doesn't it—what are the Monopoly games in *our* lives? Other than Monopoly.

In what ways are we landing on Boardwalk and *not* buying it, even though we can afford to and already have Park Place?

Or to translate this into the language of everyday experience, in what ways are we being mediocre human beings, instead of good dogs?

Hypnotism

By the time you have picked up this book, it is very likely that you have, in your life, acquired some knowledge. As our senses feed information into our brains it is inevitable that this natural occurrence should occur, and while it is lamentable, it is not the end of the world, and it is a phenomenon that can be dealt with.

Within the field of knowledge that you have acquired there will be some facts that are more damaging to your health, success, and happiness than others. Some of us will know that we'll never succeed in anything we do. Others among us will know that we're fakes. Big fat fakes, with a cushy book-deal from a publisher who's obviously just stopped caring. Others still will know that we're just naughty little smarty-pant boys who will never amount to anything and who no one will ever truly love, even if they say they do.

What Can I Do?

I'm sure right now you're saying, "But what can I do about this? Good God Man! It's no good your blithering on about the detrimental effects of knowledge if you won't give me the bally means to remedy the situation! Is there hope? Do you have a solution, for by thunder, you'd better not be wasting my time!"

There are several ways to get rid of unwanted knowledge. The healthiest way is by burying it deep within our subconsciousnesses.

For this we need a tool that I like to call, "hypnotism."

Now this might sound like an extreme measure, and there are always people who will react with skepticism.

"Hypnotism!" they'll say, "Poppycock! Boulderdash! Why ... harrumph ... Good day to you sir! ... I said good day!"

Already In Use

But hypnotism is already being used to fight many psychological and physical ailments. Trained hypnotists use hypnotistic techniques to hypnotistically help patients battle addictions; or to discover the root causes of their neuroses; even to overcome their inability to imitate chickens.

When I use hypnotism in this way I begin by placing my subject in a little trance. While in this trance I reach into their subconsciousnesses and find a repressed memory. Something they were glad to have forgotten all about. Because it's only by remembering these things, focusing on them, and reliving them, that we can truly tamp them down, stuffing them into the furthest reaches of the mind, and covering them with shovelfuls of ignorance, so they won't bother us again for at least five weeks.

An Actual Person Who Came To Me!

What follows is a transcript of a tape-recording of a hypnotical session in which I used hypnotistical techniques to cure a young man of his fear of dogs.

I have included the session in its entirety without re-reading it because I remember it all so very clearly.

Transcript begins ...

Vaguen: —essing two buttons at once! That can't be right!

Young man: It's fine, you need to press the record and the play at the same time, it's how they all work. Look, you can see the tape going round.

Vaguen: Yes it is! Well, thank you so much for that, what do I owe you?

Young man : No, I came here because you were going to help *me*. I just got the tape-recorder working because you wanted to record the session.

Vaguen: Yes, I remember, how stupid of me. Oh no, now I look like an idiot. My first paying referral and I've messed it up just by not knowing how the tape-recorder works.

Vaguen: Duh.

Vaguen: Duh.

Vaguen: Duh.

Vaguen: So, what seems to be the problem?

Young man: Er, *my* problem?

Vaguen: Yes, of course, that's why you're here isn't it?

Young man: Well, I have a bit of a phobia. I'm terrified of dogs.

Vaguen: But dogs are so cute!

Young man: Right. You know what, I think I should go. My friends were laughing when they gave me your number and now I see why ...

Vaguen: Listen, young man, I can help you. You're frightened of dogs, and that's okay. It's because of what happened when you were a child isn't it?

Young man: Yes it is. That's actually quite insightful.

Vaguen: I know all about it. A dog hurt you when you were a child and you're worried that a dog will hurt you now, that he'll disappear and you'll never see him again. And when you were a child that wasn't so bad, mummy could cheer you up by giving you that special yummy stew she always made whenever the most recent dog disappeared. And you'd see how happy she looked in her new slippers, and that made things better too, didn't it? Because you hardly ever saw her looking happy. Am I right?

Young man: No. I'm frightened because when I was a child I was bitten by a do—

Vaguen: Your problem is that you have too much knowledge.

Young man: Really?

Vaguen: Yes. You *know* that dogs hurt you, so you're frightened of them. If you didn't *know* that they could hurt you, you wouldn't be afraid. It's a classic case of the need for the Power of Ignorance.

Young man: The what?!

Vaguen: The Power of Ignorance. It's my philosophy. I give seminars on it, I'm even working on a book. I already have a publisher.

Young man: Oh yeah, I've heard about that, where they print a dud on purpose to save money on taxes.

Vaguen: Duh.

Vaguen: Duh.

Vaguen: Duh.

Young man: So what do I do?

Vaguen: You don't do anything. I'm going to hypnotize you. Once you're in a trance I'll hide all your memories of dogs hurting you. You'll then be able to continue your life worshipping them like normal people do.

Young man: Yeah, you know what? I don't think this is a good idea.

Vaguen: Woof! Woof!

Young man: What are you doing?

Vaguen: Woof! Woof! Am I frightening you?

Young man : Well, yes.

Vaguen: That's how bad your phobia is! You're even afraid of someone impersonating a dog! I can help you! Don't you want to be able to play monopoly again?!

Young man: What are you talking about? Let me go! (the sound of a door rattling) Hey, when did you lock this door?

Vaguen: Look at the watch!

Young man: What? No!

Vaguen: Yes! Watch the watch swing back and forth, back and forth. Focus on my voice.

Young man: I'm not going to look at the watch! And … you're still wearing it! You're insane!

Vaguen: I will count to five. At one you will begin to drift off the shores of consciousness. At two you will begin to drift further and faster. At three you will lose sight of land altogether, at foooouuurrr, you … will … be … asleeeee …

(pause)

Young man: Hello?

(pause)

Young man: Um, you know what? I'm really not frightened of dogs any more, I'm going to go.

(The sound of someone going through pockets, finding a key, unlocking the door, then grabbing a handful of change from a saucer before leaving.)

(The sound of breathing continues for forty minutes.)

…Transcript ends

As we can see, that young man's phobia was cured in a single session. I never had to see him again, but I got many referrals from him, often people who had no problems but who he felt 'should just check this guy out.'

Chapter 8
Inspiration Is Ninety-Nine Percent Ignorance And One Percent Sweat

In this chapter we will look at the Power of Ignorance and inspiration.

The Wright Brothers

Probably the most famous example of the Power of Ignorance is the Wright Brothers. Now, I know what you're thinking, "the Wright Brothers?" "Ignorance?" "Denver?"

Let me explain. At the end of the 18th century, scientists all over the world were racing to be the first to discover the secret of "Heavier Than Air Flight." Orville and Wilbur Wright didn't have a lot of money—they weren't even formally trained, but what they did have was *ignorance*.

You see the first step the brothers took when they began their work was to throw out all the existing knowledge and research on how flight would be achieved; thus proceeding from a position of ignorance.

As we know they succeeded in achieving "Heavier Than Air Flight" while their better-funded, more established contemporaries were quite literally *not achieving* it.

That's a pretty inspiring true story of the Power of Ignorance.

What Is Inspiration?

But just what is inspiration? What does it mean to be inspired?

The dictionary definition of inspiration is *Denkanstoss*; *Anregung*; *Eingebung*, but this tells us nothing.

If we look at the entomology of the word we see that it comes from the Latin "inspiratio" meaning "to breathe in," but it's probably best if we don't think about breathing at all . . .

YOU GOT ME HORNED OUT HONEY
GIRL I'M FEELIN FUNNY
YOU'RE WELCOME TO SEE WHAT WE'VE
BEEN DOIN IN MY DREAMS
YOU PUT A CURSE ON ME SUGAR
ALL I WANT TO DO IS HOOK UP WICH'U

Perhaps the best way to find what inspiration truly *means* is to look at what it *does*.

Perceptions

An inspiring story changes our perceptions of what we think we're capable of by providing us with an example of someone overcoming similar obstacles. In their story we see that the Wright Bros overcame their lack of resources with ignorance. If you're facing a task that you assume you're not qualified for, or well enough equipped for, then this story might enable you to continue confidently.

Our Bodies

When faced with a problem we perceive as insurmountable our bodies react negatively. Our shoulders hunch, our necks become tense. We get angry very quickly, and our eyes dart from side to side. Usually we'll start to giggle, initially at times when laughter would be acceptable, only we'll do it a little too much and for a few seconds too long. Then we'll giggle at times when laughter isn't acceptable. Gradually the giggling becomes non-stop while we're speaking, and finally spreads to when we're not speaking too.

Now let's look at a situation where again we're faced with a difficult problem, but this time we've just heard about someone else's success in a similar situation. Our tension eases, we stand straighter. Our voices become smoother, more commanding, and we hardly ever lash out at someone, perhaps a child, asking us how things are going.

Deciding Factor

The changes that come about because we know that what we're faced with is not impossible are so great that they may be the deciding factor in our own success.

Imagine facing a difficult job interview giggling, rubbing your hands together and whispering "yessssss . . . Yessss!!!!" whenever the person interviewing you is speaking. I don't think you'll be getting your name on one of those prestigious nametags anytime soon!

Now imagine facing the same job interview tall, calm-eyed and self assured. Looks like someone better clear his schedule! (Because the interview was a success and they've offered you the job.)

But, But, But . . .

"But what does this have to do with ignorance?" you might ask. (But you don't have to.)

Well, let's see if we can find a connection when we look at a few more examples.

Wilbur Wright Again

When Wilbur Wright was just fourteen years old, he sustained terrible head injuries in an accident while playing an early primitive form of ice hockey.

The doctors told his parents that based on their *knowledge* and experience, they *knew* that Wilbur would never recover, that he would never again read, write, or think, and that any attempt to rehabilitate him would actually make things worse.

His parents decided to *ignore* this knowledge, and proceed from a position of ignorance, and Wilbur as we know wasn't just rehabilitated, he went on to become one of the most important scientific minds of his or any other century.

Very Inspiring

Now that is a very inspiring story of the Power of Ignorance. It's even more inspiring than the first story. It's also a *lie*.

But think about it. Wasn't the story more inspiring when you *didn't know* it was a lie?

Yes it was.

Just think what you could have achieved if you had had this fictitious "Wilbur Wright" as a role model. You could have done anything.

"If Wilbur Wright could recover from his head injuries," you would say "surely I can overcome my fears and program this brand new VCR!"

You can find this and many other untrue inspiring stories in my soon to be published companion book, *Chicken Soup for the Ignorant Soul*.

Scratch

But making up a story from scratch like that is only one way to provide yourself with inspiration.

I'd like to share with you now a success story from the world of movies. And this one is true and I haven't altered it a bit.

A Little Boy

Many years ago a little boy decided that of all the activities at his school, the thing he enjoyed most was acting in the school plays. He joined the drama club and was always one of the major cast members in school productions. Everyone knew he loved acting, and there was no surprise when he left high school to study drama in University.

Four years later that little boy was a bright-eyed, excited young actor living in New York, doing the usual round of acting in community theatre, leaving his resume with agents and attending open calls for Broadway shows. He spent several years in this way, struggling to make ends meet, performing all kinds of odd-jobs.

No Skills

This man has recently told people that one of the things that made him stick to his dream was that he had no skills other than acting, and so was never tempted to give it all up and become a successful businessman, because he wouldn't even have been able to get an interview, let alone beat several infinitely better-qualified applicants.

He struggled in this way for *ten more years*, always sticking to his dream of being an actor, working as an extra for a few dollars a day and a free meal, even teaching himself to juggle so that he could busk on the street, collecting those precious pennies to pay for his expensive juggling equipment.

Never Gave Up

But through all this hardship he never gave up; not when he couldn't afford to fly home for his grandmother's funeral, not when he lived on the street for three months, not even when one prospective agent who saw him in a community theatre production of Macbeth told him, "You are the most talentless ham I've ever fallen asleep to." He went on to say, "And if you ever contact me again I will hunt you down and kill you. Slowly."

This actor kept his dream alive because deep down, he knew that he would make it.

Do you want to know his name?

Are you sure?

Well alright, his name is . . .

Terry Norton.

He's the assistant manager at a video store around the corner from me.

John Malkovich

But what if his name had been John Malkovich? You would have come away from that story convinced that determination was all you needed to make your dreams come true. Before you *knew* the name of the actor in the story you were much happier and more confident.

Odds

For any story of success over the odds, there will by definition be stories of failure. The very reason the odds are "a million to one" is that for every one success there are a corresponding 999,999 failures. Try not to think about that next time you succeed! You're dooming thousands of others to failure! Way to go, successful guy! Thanks a lot!

For everyone who ever got the courage to tell their boss the truth and gained a promotion there are a dozen out-of-work businessmen. Maybe even a *baker's* dozen. For every dream followed to success there are a hundred that turn into nightmares. And the higher the odds against you, the more stories of failure there will be.

But how does *knowing* about those failures inspire you?

It is far better to allow yourself to be inspired by one story of success than to burden yourself with the knowledge of exactly how rare those successes are.

An ability to bend reality, to choose ignorance of those facts that don't suit your purposes, along with ignorance of the knowledge that the facts you do use are entirely wrong, is one of the most powerful tools you will ever have in your attempt to achieve a can-do attitude.

Another Example

Let's look at another example.

A little boy spent the first part of his life as an undernourished youth on the streets of San Francisco. He suffered from rickets, a disease caused by lack of vitamin D, which made him bow-legged. Now no one would say that he had life handed to him on a silver spoon! No one would have blamed him if he'd given up and settled for a life of "if only"s, citing his many disadvantages as his perfectly viable reasons for going nowhere.

But he didn't give up. He made his life work for him, pushing himself harder and harder to excellence, eventually becoming world famous as a sportsman, then an actor. He changed his name from the strange and easily mocked Orenthal to the far more punchy "OJ Simpson."

Genuinely Inspiring

In this case the story is genuinely inspiring; we just want to get rid of the *knowledge* that it's a story about a man who some people believe to be a murderous, abusive, hyper-controlling maniac.

Beautiful Quote

"A meeting between two people who complete each other, who are made for each other, borders already, in my opinion, on a miracle."—Gandhi

That's a beautiful quote, as anyone would agree. It speaks of an abiding love of love itself, and a respect for love as a powerful force in the world that we should all take the responsibility of nurturing wherever we find it. When most people read or hear the quote they experience a tingling warmth and a sense of hope in the future. Women will sigh and men will blink back tears, pretending they had allergies.

But that wonderful feeling disappears when they find out that it wasn't Gandhi who said the quote; it was Adolf Hitler.

A tiny change in reality is all that's needed to return those good feelings.

"A meeting between two people who complete each other, who are made for each other, borders already, in my opinion, on a miracle."—Adolf Hitler

"I wish I'd said that."—Gandhi

Try this yourself.

"Nothing in the world is as important as family."—Charles Manson

You can remove the creepy overtones from this quote by attributing it to, well let's face it—anyone else. You might also want to avoid known mafia figures. And anyone called Oedipus.

?

Achievements Of Other People

As we have seen, applying ignorance to stories of the achievements of other people is a wonderful way to make those stories more inspiring.

But why just be inspired by the achievements of others?

It's so much more powerful when you can be inspired by the achievements of . . . yourself.

People who have overcome incredible odds will often say that afterwards everything else seemed easy.

"I climbed Mount Everest" they would say. "Surely I can change the ink cartridge in this printer!"

But the wonderful thing is, you don't have to climb Mount Everest to benefit from this phenomenon. All you have to do is forget the knowledge that you never have.

The Next Time You Find Yourself

The next time you find yourself in a difficult situation, simply say, "Aren't I the same person who crash-landed in that plane and had to crawl twenty miles through jungle carrying my own severed head? Surely I can peel this orange even though I've just trimmed my fingernails! Didn't I program that VCR? Well surely I can perform this triple-bypass surgery."

Key

Ignorance is a key part of any success story.

Successful people when asked will always say things like:

"I don't know the meaning of the word 'quit'" or "I don't know what fear is" or "The words 'I can't do this' aren't in my dictionary."

Vocabulary Of Failure

By using the Power of Ignorance, you too can expand your lack of knowledge of the vocabulary of failure.

Just think what you could achieve if you didn't know the meaning of the words, "quit," "fail," "stop that," "it's illegal you know," "gravity always goes down." "If it didn't work the last nine times, and you're not changing anything you're doing, what makes you think it'll work this time?"

Why, if I hadn't rid myself of the knowledge of the meaning of the words "Your philosophy is absurd and you'll never be a successful motivational speaker," then you wouldn't be reading this book. *My* book.

Don't Know Thyself

People say "Know thyself!!!!" They're wrong.

How often, when we examine ourselves, when we look deep, deep inside, do we not like what we find? Every time.

Try it just for a second. Hold your breath and take a glance at what's inside of you.

Look at that stuff. Yecccccccch!! All gooey and red and sticky and stringy and raw and gross.

Try shedding that image from your mind now that you've seen it. Good luck! You can't! I'll bet you wish you'd never seen any of that stuff! You quite certainly wish you hadn't gotten to know thyself!

If you don't examine thy(your)self, if you don't know your(thy)self, what are you left with? The surface. The pleasant mask you assume to deal with the big cruel world. That mask knows how to cope. That mask always smiles. That mask can at least pretend to get along with pretty much anyone.

Well what's so bad about that??? Sounds like a nice guy to me!

A Perfect Stool

Many people think of ignorance as something simple, and easy to achieve. Well, this isn't necessarily the case. It does lie within us, but only with careful cultivation can it emerge as a thing of beauty. Like a perfect stool.

Picture a stool. A stool's a very useful thing. You can sit on it and enjoy a cold drink. You can stand on it to reach a high shelf. Three or four stools piled in front of the breakfast nook can present a very attractive picture.

Now those stools didn't just spring into existence. Each one was crafted by a living, breathing, human being.

Picture the man who's just made that stool. You know, the stool you were picturing only a moment ago. Imagine he's just completed its creation. See the look of satisfaction on his face, inspecting the thing he's made. He might stare at it for quite a while, marvelling that such a thing came into the world because of him. Look as he might, he can't find a single flaw in it.

Is a stool easy to make? Possibly. Anyone can sequester themselves for an hour or two and crank out a stool, it's true. Given they had the raw materials in the first place. And the tools. And a place to do it in.

But would that then be an attractive stool? Would it be the kind you'd be proud to put in the middle of your living room, in a coveted spot on the carpet? Would you bring friends over to look at it? Would you draw their attention to it, saying things like "Look at that stool"? And when they remarked "Now that's an impressive stool" would you then remark "I made that stool. All by myself"?

No, you would not. At least, probably not. Because they wouldn't have made their remark. They'd be embarrassed to see such a thing. They'd avert their eyes. They'd pretend it wasn't there, dominating the room, radiating its eminence to the point where it couldn't be ignored anymore. It would be an ugly, shameful, disgusting thing which no one would feel good about resting their feet upon. Instead of standing directly on it, people would step around it and warn others to do so as well.

But now consider a man who takes the time he needs to craft his stool. He knows you can't rush a perfect creation. He'll devote the entire day to it, no matter what anyone in his family says. He'll apply himself like the artisan he has every right to consider himself.

Hours later, he'll emerge, perhaps somewhat shaken in appearance, his strength drained from his mighty endeavor. But he'll beam with pride. He'll wear a smile that only such an occasion could evoke from his face—a smile of rejuvenation. He'll hold that stool aloft with pride, perhaps donning gloves, perhaps resting it on a special cushion. He'll put it in a place of honour. He'll be sure to make it the focal point of whichever room he leaves it in.

And every time he sees it, he'll think to himself "Now that's a handsome stool. And I made it. Oh yes I did." And he'll keep it firmly in his sight as he steps right onto it and stands there. He'll stand there for as long as he likes. And then the memory of that stool will stay with him for the rest of the day as he walks around town. Others will sense it, and ask him about it. And he'll tell them. You won't be able to shut him up about it.

That's what true ignorance is like.

Chapter 9
Admit Your Ignorance

If You Don't Know Something, Admit It!

There's a general perception that not knowing something is a sign of weakness. For some reason people think that being ignorant is bad. This stigma attached to ignorance, (otherwise known as a "stigmarence") is unfortunate indeed. It can lead to easily avoidable trouble.

Asking for Directions

Stereotypically, adult men are reticent to ask for directions while driving. Even when they *know* they're lost, they'd rather soldier on, pretending they know where they're going.

If the possibility of being lost is mentioned to them, this only strengthens their resolve.

"I know where I'm going!!"

"I've driven here a hundred times!!"

"Why do they make the street signs so hard to see!!"

"When did they move the old schoolhouse!! It used to be on the other side of the street!!"

"Shut!! Up!!"

"I wish I'd never married you!! If I hadn't knocked you up with that brat strapped onto the roof I'd be long gone!!"

Supremely

These men are ignorant—and supremely so—*and there's nothing wrong with that*—but they won't admit it.

If they'd only own up to the fact that they don't know every last road in the world, they'd get to their destinations much faster.

"Excuse me, I'm not from around here. Could you tell me how to get to (fill in the blank destination)?"

"I'm certainly glad you asked me, sir. Because I *am* from around here and I know how to get where you're going. And given that you're from somewhere else there's no shame in you *not* knowing. Allow me to give you detailed directions which you'll find easy to follow."

"Thank you. Hear that son? This kind man knows where the bookstore is. We'll be there in no time."

"Yippee!"

"Why, that's a fine young man you have there. Like to read, do you?"

"Yippee!"

"Well, I could never let a fellow bookworm go by without giving him one of these."

"Look daddy! It's a gift certificate for twenty dollars at the bookstore where we're headed! Yippee!"

"Yippee!"

"Yippee!"

"Yippee!"

That's the kind of exchange that would be common in a world where no one was ashamed to admit their ignorance.

?

Ignorant Millionaires

In fact, if you're willing to admit you don't know everything about everything it can not only prevent frustration and unhappiness, it can make you wealthy beyond your wildest imaginings.

Andrew Carnegie, J. Pierpont Morgan, Henry Rockefeller—these aren't made up clown names—they're actually the names of a couple of famously wealthy businessmen. And yet every single one of them realized and then capitalized on their own ignorance.

Andrew Carnegie

Andrew Carnegie earned the bulk of his wealth in the steel

industry. He never worked in a steel mine. He never worked in a steel mill. He never visited building sites that used his steel. He was the first to admit he was no authority on the subject. "Let me say right here and now," he would begin every conversation, "I don't know *spit* about steel."

JP Morgan was a railroad magnate. He proudly admitted "I hardly even know what a train is, but I'm strangely drawn to them."

Rockefeller, founder of Standard Oil, once said "Huh? Oil?! I thought we sold combs! No one tells me nuffin', 'cause I'm full of straw."

How did these men amass fortunes in fields they blabbed to anyone and everyone they knew nothing about? They admitted their own ignorance and then hired people who *did* know.

These learned experts worked for them. They were paid well and their expertise was never questioned. Their knowledge promptly filled their boss's pockets and bank accounts (with money). When the experts' brains went dry the bosses hired more experts, who earned them more money with which they hired more experts, and so on and so on and so on. Before you knew it, they were rich.

So who needs knowledge? It didn't do those experts any good. They're all dead.

?

Dear Vaguen

The following is a letter I received from a seminar attendee in Saskatoon.

> I was being considered by my superiors for a job that had become known amongst my co-workers and me as "the widow-maker." The last four men who'd had it had lasted less than a year before being fired. And yet all of us wanted it. Why? Because all of the company's top execs had been groomed in that very position.
>
> Success in it meant a one-way ticket to the top.

Failure meant unemployment and humiliation.

It wasn't a job given over casually. Whoever got it would need to know every department, every client, every aspect of the business, and a whole lot else, besides.

Studied

I studied for my chance. I put in long hours for months. I met with every department head and kept notes on everything I found out. I carried these notes around with me on index cards and studied them on the train to and from work.

You'd think this would help, but it only ended up showing me how much there was to know, and what a small fraction of it I had a handle on.

As my interview got closer, I was sure down in the dumps. My plan had backfired. Before, I thought I'd known what I was doing. Now I knew I was just a stupe. But who knows—I'd picked up a fair bit of jargon, and could name-drop like nobody's business! Why not bluff 'em?

Interview

When my interview came up I stood before the board as if on trial for my life.

The twelve board members stared at me. The CEO cleared his throat. I don't want to be crude, but I almost wet myself.

"So, what makes you think you, of all cotton-pickin' people, are the right man for this job" he said as a casual opener. It was worded as a question but sounded more like an accusation. That's probably why he didn't use a question mark.

I was on the point of giving him the elaborate spiel I'd concocted, but at the last second something took ahold of me and I looked at them all and said:

"You know, I'm *not* ready. I wish I was. I know

a lot about this business, but not everything, and the impression I get is that this job needs more than I've accumulated so far. But thanks for considering me. I hope you don't feel I've wasted your time, but I thought it was important to be honest with you."

Dramatic Pause

There was a dramatic pause as the board exchanged surprised looks.

Suddenly the room burst into hearty laughter and applause. The chairman looked strangely moved. He stood up, walked around the large boardroom table, and shook my hand.

"Congratulations, son" he said "Everyone else tried to pull one over on us but we caught 'em all in their own lies. But you admitted your ignorance."

"Someone as honest as you has a great future in our company. Our whole business rests on our rich clients trusting that we know what we're doing."

He handed me a cigar. And we all laughed and laughed and laughed.

Secret

I'm now in a secret executive management training program. The plan is that I'll thoroughly learn every department from the bottom up. I've been mopping floors for seven years, but I guess I don't know everything about cleaning because there's no sign of me moving departments yet!

I know I'm going to fit in well when I eventually get to the top because the execs always point and laugh when they see me.

"Look!" they say "It's the honest guy!"

And who wouldn't want to be called that?

I'm sure my now ex-wife is looking forward to me getting to the top too.

?

Yanking Out the Credibility Rug

Perhaps the worst aspect of denying your ignorance is when someone catches you in it. It ends up casting doubt in their mind on everything they've ever heard you say. They would end up not believing anything. Including things that you were completely right about!

Have you ever been in a relationship that's turned suddenly sour, and then ended quite badly just two years later? You'll find that even the happy memories are tainted with the vision of smacks on the nose with a newspaper, a deep voice telling you exactly what's wrong with you over and over again as the flames from your favourite encyclopedia dry the tears before they can even leave your eyes.

It's a bit like that.

Jittery

A while ago I had the delightful experience of being approached by an old college buddy.

"Hey hey hey hey hey, Vaguen! Over here!

"Hey Vaguen, remember when we were in that loonie bin together?"

I agreed with him that our university had been something of a madhouse. And he resumed his story.

"Yeah, I remember now, you thought you wuz . . . Aaaaw what they heck! Lemme tellya something Vaguen. I like you. I know what you've been through. My mother was a real piece of work too.

"All the time I was growing up my mom couldn't admit that she didn't know something. Anything. Anything you asked her about, anything anyone was talking about. You name it, she knew more about it than you. She was the authority. She knew what there was to know, end of story. If she didn't know it, it was wrong.

"Now I was a kid, right, so I asked her questions all of the time.

'Mom, why is the sky blue?'
'What makes the tide go in and out?'
'Why do bears hibernate?'
'What's the capital of Brazil?'
'How do they make paper?'

"I was a curious kid, what can I say? Anyways, my mom shot back an answer for every question I had. 'Because it's a reflection of the sea.' 'Because of the salt.' 'Because they're too fat to trudge through the snow.' 'Toronto.' 'By pressing hard on wood.'

"I loved it. She knew everything.

"You had to be careful though. Only so many questions in a day. Too many and . . . watch out!

Years Later

"Years later, my science teacher told me an interesting tidbit when we were studying astronomy, or physics or something. She said if all the gravity and the air disappeared not only would things float around all over the place, but our bodies would explode. Yeah, that's right, they'd EXPLODE. She actually said that.

"She told us it's the earth's gravitational and atmospheric pressure that keeps us in the physical shapes we're in, and if that pressure lifted, we'd expand in all directions. KABOOM!

"I couldn't believe it.

"I raised my hand.

"'Is that why astronauts need to wear spacesuits instead of just breath masks?' I asked.

"'That's right' she said.

"I was goddam-well glowing for getting that one right.

"'Also' she went on 'in space the blood from our exploding bodies would be blue. A lot of the blood that flows through our veins is blue. Only when it comes in contact with oxygen does it instantly turn red.'

"'So a spaceman who took off his helmet would . . . explode . . . blue?'

"'Exactly'"

"As outrageous as this sounded, it came from a science teacher. She pulled out a few reference books from behind her desk and passed them to me, showing me the parts that backed up what she'd just said.

"I ran home. I couldn't wait to tell my mom about this!

Mom, Listen!

"'Mom, listen to this! If there was no gravity, guess what would happen!'

"'Things would float around.'

"'Not only that—we'd all EXPLODE!'

She looked at me and shook her head.

"'No—it's true! And if the air went too, our blood would be blue!'

"She led me to the garage and gave me the caning of my life."

Regained

"A couple of hours later I stood at my desk, for once happy that I'd never been given a chair.

"I started thinking about all the things my mom had told me over the years about how things worked. I couldn't trust anything she'd ever told me.

"I went back to science class and asked my teacher if some of the other stuff my mom had told me was true. She couldn't have been more wrong, it turned out. Everyone laughed and laughed. At me! For having believed that bunk!

"My mom, I realized, was full of . . ."

At this my jittery friend stopped his story and looked from side to side. When he was satisfied that no one was looking at us he continued . . .

"She was full of . . . THE 'S' WORD!
"I never trusted her again."

At this point, my old university chum dived under a table. I joined him as he finished his story.

Yanking Off

"Years later, I became an astronaut. And when I was on the moon even though some part of me wanted to, I stopped myself from yanking off my helmet. Even though I had a breathmask with me.

"My mother became an astronaut too, you know. We were walking on the moon together, and I reached over and wrenched off her helmet! And she exploded blue! She was a disgusting blue mess! Ah ha ha ha ha ha!!!

"When I got back to the rocket the other astronauts wanted to know where she was and I said 'I thought she was with you!'

"We flew back without her.

"I got back to earth just fine, thank you very much and was awarded a trophy for Best Human Being. It came with a million dollars.

"Yeah! So, ignorance, man! You got it!"

He then placed his finger in his ear and shook it vigourously for five minutes.

He hadn't changed a bit.

?

So?

What these examples show us is that far from helping us, hiding our ignorance can have very damaging effects on our well-beings.

But admitting our ignorance will allow us to achieve our goals, be they as simple as finding a bookstore, gaining the respect of our co-workers, or earning millions of dollars. Or the admittedly rarer benefit of *not* exploding in space because of our son's quite reasonable anger built up over years and years of lies and unfair treatment by a mummy who just didn't know what it was to love anything.

So there you go.

Chapter 10
Nobody Likes A Smartass

Silence is Nice

Once I saw a small placard on the wall of an office cubicle that said "The Only Acceptable Substitute For Brains Is Silence."

"Silence!"

"Brains!"

"SUBSTITUTE!"

Once I picked myself up off the floor and wiped away the tears of hysterical laugher, I realized that this bit of office humour is quite right. If you don't say anything, how can you be wrong?

Emanates From Someone

The most genuine silence is that which emanates from someone who has absolutely nothing to say. And the person who has nothing to say isn't just someone who doesn't value their own opinions, it's someone who doesn't *have* opinions. Because they don't think anything at all. Think of how much better a place the world would be if troublemakers and mean people had nothing in their heads whatsoever? They'd actually be quite pleasant.

Even Better Than Silence

The only thing that makes a silent, ignorant person even more pleasant and easy to be around is if they wear a smile. All the time. Regardless of how they feel. After all, a smile is not only nice to look at, but, if held long enough, it projects an infinite amount of ignorance.

What If I'm Sad?

Ah, but I hear you asking already "Hey dude, what if I'm sad?"

What if I'm angry, man? What if like, the blue meanies are gettin' me down and there ain't no way up to happy town?"

Easy. Smile anyway. A smile is a simple physiological pose of the facial muscles. It might appear naturally when you're happy, the way you might instinctually jump if the ground you stood on suddenly caught fire. But if that ground stayed room temperature you'd still be able to jump. You'd just have to decide to do it. And would that jump look any less like an organic jump because it hadn't sprung from any real need to jump? No it wouldn't. It would be a perfect simulation of a jump. Hardly anyone would be able to distinguish it from a genuine jump.

Who Cares?

So who cares how hot or cold the ground is? Smile, dammit! Plaster a great big smile clear across your face and keep it there all day. Make it as big as you can. Arch and extend your eyebrows. Open your mouth. Open your jaw. Feel your face turn red from the muscular exertion of it all. What a feeling! Do you notice how it strains? What a difference there is between a natural smile and one we choose to make. The latter requires ten times the energy. Your face muscles make sure you know about it too. That's exercise! It's good for you! So keep that smile big, and consistent. Good. Now walk around like that. I said WALK AROUND!

Common Exchange

Take a look at this common exchange between a grocer and a customer.

"Oh. Hello."
"Hi"
"Can you tell me where the apples are?"
"They're over there"
"Thank you"
(pause)
"I'd like to buy these apples, please"
"That'll be $2.99"

"Here you go"
"Have a nice day"
"You too"

Hideous isn't it? Feel the tension and underlying hatred. You could light it with a match.

But let's see what happens when Sammy Smile enters the room!

"Oh. Hello"
"(GRIN!)"
"Can . . . uh . . . can you tell me where the apples are?"
"(GRIN!)"
"Never mind, I see them."
(pause)
"I'd like to buy these apples, please"
"(GRIN!)"
"Uhh . . . are you all right?"
"(GRIN!)"
"So, I see these are $2.99?"
"(GRIN!)"
"Here's a twenty."
"(GRIN!)"
" . . . "
"(GRIN!)"
" . . . "
"(GRIN!)"
"Tell you what . . . uh . . . keep the change. I'm getting out of here."
"(GRIN!)"

The second grocer was much more pleasant to be around, and his sunny disposition even earned him a fat tip!

Eat More Fruit

Who would argue that the second example is a picture of a better world? And if anyone did argue that point, wouldn't a tremendous sustained smile directed at them for an hour or so be all it took to win them over? Why, if everyone smiled all the time, we wouldn't have arguments, nasty feelings, or wars. Sounds like a good world to me! And it can all start with a smile.

And don't think from the above example that only people in the grocery store will feel the benefit of your smile. You'll notice the difference it makes in your interactions with everyone who crosses your path. Even those you have no reason to interact with, like the people walking past you on the sidewalk, or the person you sit next to on the bus.

Creep

Ordinarily these people wouldn't register your existence at all. But they will now!

Your broad gaping grin will stay with them, I promise you. They'll talk about you at work. They'll describe you to their families as they watch TV. Try as they might they won't be able to forget you. Images of your massive smiling mouth will creep into their minds' eyes as they lie in bed. They might even find themselves unconsciously making sculptures of your face in their mashed potatoes.

And what do you know, before long they'll be sporting billboard sized smiles of their own, yelping for joy to the world whether they want to or not. At all times!

So smile all day and all night. Join the happy, ignorant revolution.

?

The Likeable Boss

Arnold Richter owned and ran a successful garment factory in Kansas City, Manitoba. He'd started the company forty years before with just himself and occasional help from one part-time worker.

From the beginning Arnold had been involved in every aspect of the work. Nothing was beneath him and he'd quite often run straight from a business meeting with an important prospective client back to the factory to sweep the floors.

As the company grew, Arnold added more staff, but always insisted on being part of every department. He had to know every aspect of every decision being made and demanded constant reports.

And that's exactly where things started to go horribly wrong.

His Staff

His staff began to resent always having to explain every decision and action they made and took. No one felt trusted in their positions or fulfilled in their work. New, potentially better ways of accomplishing a task were routinely quashed, as Arnold kept his employees strictly within the limits of how he *knew* everything should be done. He was convinced that his ways were the only ways if the company was to stay healthy.

The more he micro-managed the more his staff hated him. And he knew this, and tripled his vigilance, now fearing deliberately shoddy work or even sabotage.

Turning Point

The turning point came when Arnold intercepted a note from one employee to another. It was a crudely drawn cartoon of Arnold giving lessons in being cruel and domineering to Hitler. And calling him "Adolf *Soft*-ler"!

Arnold looked at himself in the mirror and didn't like what he saw.

"How did this happen?" He asked plaintively.

To his surprise, the mirror replied.

"Screw you, buddy!" it said, "Why don't you go kill yourself. That'll make the world happy, you hyper-controlling bastard!"

Suspicious, Arnold looked behind the mirror to see another one of his unhappy employees.

"I mean it! Kill yourself!" said the man and ran out into the hallway.

Didn't Know

He didn't know what to do. He idly flipped through the newspaper and saw a notice for one of **MY** seminars which said "Don't know? Good!" He put down the newspaper and left immediately.

Let me tell you, I've never known so enthusiastic a student. After a mere one hour session, he shook my hand vigourously and promised to apply everything he'd learned immediately.

Did

And that's exactly what he did. He stopped trying to know everything that was going on and instead spent his time encouraging and empowering everyone who worked for him. When people came to him with a problem he would simply look them in the eye and say "I trust your judgment on this one. Whatever you decide to do, I'll back you one hundred percent."

It didn't take long for his employees to love him. He knew things had turned around one day when he picked up a note carelessly dropped by a secretary—a cartoon of himself gently reprimanding Jesus for not being nice enough. And calling him "*Mean*-sus Christ."

Crowning Moment

The crowning moment of his life came six months later, when his entire staff forfeited their final paycheques in order to throw him a party to console him for the liquidation of all his assets. Tearful choruses of "For He's a Jolly Good Fellow" rang in his ears and heart as he was turned out into the street, the building padlocked behind him.

If he had still been trying to run every department, assuming he knew better than everyone there, I don't think his staff would have been anywhere near as generous.

?

Everyone Loves a Listener

Not knowing things can make you an excellent listener.

For instance, a young man—Richard Benjamin by name—who'd taken one of my seminars applied this principal when he was sent to the office of a Mr. Coleman, the regional director of a large construction company. Richard had to win the contract to carpet a large housing development Coleman's company was building.

This powerful man had been in the same office for twenty-five years. He was a notoriously hard man, known to keep an egg-timer on his desk and limit all interviews to five minutes.

The contract was for millions of dollars, and if Richard didn't get it, his company's future was well nigh kaput. He had five minutes and no more.

Noticed

Richard walked into that office and noticed what must have been dozens of model airplanes hanging from fishing line so thin you could barely see it.

"Say," he said, "that's some pretty transparent fishing line!"

"Isn't it though?" said Coleman, brightening up like a sunflower. "I bought it all myself."

"I've always wanted to know more about fishing line, but I must confess I just don't."

Coleman beamed.

"My son, pull up a chair."

Three Hours

Coleman regaled the young man not for five minutes but for two hours! He told Richard all about his first encounters with fishing line. He described how he'd learned to love it so much, and how it made him feel to hang things from it, and to not quite see it all around him.

Richard could tell Coleman was having the best day of work he'd ever had.

What Coleman Didn't Know

What Coleman didn't know was that Richard couldn't possibly have been less interested in fishing line. In fact he hated the stuff! He thought Coleman a fool and a nut. But this didn't come across. Why not? Because he was smiling and nodding the whole time. Coleman was so enraptured with his own interest, he hardly even needed Richard to be there!

Smiling And Patting

After three exhausting hours Coleman showed him out, smiling and patting him on the back.

"We haven't talked about the contract at all," Richard said.

"Don't worry about it," Coleman replied. "I think we've spent our time well."

He grasped his hand in a warm handshake and winked at him.

Guess Who Won The Contract

Here is a riddle. See if you can guess it. When the time came to award the carpeting contract, which company do you think got it? No, no. You're wrong. Guess again. No, that's wrong too. Oh, the hell with it, I'll just tell you.

It was Hoggenton Tweed, another company with a lower price and a superior product.

Richard himself was fired when his board of directors found out how he'd squandered his sales pitch meeting.

Richard may have lost a job (and later a house and a marriage), but he'd found a friend. And that Christmas, Coleman's secretary sent him a Christmas card. And in the envelope next to that card was a foot-long piece of fishing line.

?

Fight

How many people get in a fight when they first meet? Boxers, perhaps, but not many of the rest of us.

People will forgive, or not even notice, the wildest deviations from their own opinions when they come from someone they hardly know at all. They'd never be so rude as to cut down a stranger. Only when a person's familiar do their minds start combing over the other person, finding imperfections and dwelling on them, brooding, giving accusing looks until their complaints come pouring out of them in a torrent like lava spilling out of a swimming pool (which had been foolishly built on top of a volcano).

Civil Relations

The better you *know* someone, the better idea you have of where to stick the knife, and how to *twist* it. And just which of their childhood fears to throw back in their face. Wouldn't all of our interactions be so much more civil if none of us *knew* each other well enough to do that?

Aren't people more interesting when you first meet them? Picture the first date between two people. They're both on their best behaviour. They're well dressed and well groomed. They're attentive to each other's stories. They're eager to laugh at each others' jokes. And most importantly: *they don't know that much about each other.*

A Woman

One time, a woman came up to me after one of my seminars.

"You're very interesting" she told me.

I thanked her politely. You see, I *didn't know* her, so I resorted to automatic courtesy. After all, she could be anyone.

She shook my hand, and looked at me. She had blue eyes and brown, curly hair, down past her shoulders.

"My name is Teresa," she told me.

"It's nice to meet you," I replied. "Where are you from?"

"Why," she answered, "right here in Denver."

The exchange was one of the most pleasant experiences in my life up until that point. I could not help but compare our brief conversation with a past interaction with a woman

I'd first met in similar circumstances, whose *knowledge* of me, and more importantly her extensive *knowledge* of all my many faults, allowed her to spend a whole half-hour shouting at me on a bus. And she hit me on the nose.

The difference? Ignorance..

Tools

There are many ways of ridding yourself of unwanted knowledge. Keep in mind the unused portion of the brain is plentiful, and there's ample room in there for everything you don't want to think about. But how can you get it there? Here are my suggestions:

1. Alcohol

This magical substance decreases what you know with every gulp. Have you ever woken up after a night of serious drinking and not remembered what you were up to after a certain point the night before? Have you ever been regaled with tales of your own drunken adventures, without having them ring the slightest bell? Consistent use of alcohol can make this an everyday experience. In fact after a certain point your whole past will be nothing but a great big happy blur. And all the aching, moaning and vomiting in the mornings will prevent you from thinking about anything then either.

2. Drugs

Why dwell on all of the miserable failures that you call your life? With the right drugs you can instead be captivated for hours and hours by the appearance of your hand. Ordinary objects or figures of speech become unbelievably funny. An otherwise unremarkable piece of music can envelop your consciousness altogether. While living in the magical fairyland that only you can see, you needn't think about a single thing. Even if you wanted to think—good luck! An erasing mechanism very similar to the lapping and retreating surf will regularly give you a clean slate upon which to ponder complete nonsense.

3. Constant Distraction

Do you know how a child (or even an adult!) will prevent themselves from being told something they don't want to hear by plugging their ears, closing their eyes, and singing a nonsense song? Technology allows us (encourages us!) to make this our natural state. Why think when there are pretty flickering lights you could be looking at, driving rhythms to listen to at high volume and aliens to be killed with the maniacal pressing of a bunch of buttons? Twenty-four hours a day, too. If this isn't enough, get a job. Join a few committees. Follow celebrity gossip. Have kids.

4. Smacking Solid Objects With Your Head

This method is tremendously effective. Of course you may be knocked insensible, and this is should be considered a prized state. Have you ever seen an unconscious person? There's a peaceful look on their face you won't find anywhere else. And remember, unconscious means "not thinking." Even once they wake up there's a prolonged period of disorientation before they remember where they are, who they are, and why they're lying on the floor.

A Lifetime

Of course it is difficult to undo the habits of a lifetime. Unwanted knowledge has a nasty tendency of lingering in the mind, like an old rotten foot that just won't fall off.

You may find things from your past—incidents, images, sentences, or even just key words popping up in your head like bubbles on the surface of the ocean. Over and over and over again. They may slip into your speech without you even realizing it.

Persevere! If you continue a regimented program of the above techniques you'll reach a stage where you'll forget what these repeated motifs even mean. And as such, you won't even notice them! They'll fade into the background of your notice like old, weathered garden gnomes the weeds have almost entirely covered up. Like a dust bunny under the bed. Like belches from a half-eaten Denver omelet.

True Power

The true Power of Ignorance lies in the very institution held so dear to us in the western world: democracy.

The entire concept of democracy is that anyone and everyone has the right to influence, or even run the country in which they happen to have been born.

Does education qualify you for a vote? No. Does wealth or social position? No. Does a strong, reasonable or even tenuous grasp of the issues? Not at all. The only thing needed is to be breathing.

What a victory for ignorance this is! Picture all of the educated, wealthy, socially positioned, and informed-on-the-issues people watch helplessly as the masses who know nothing at all rise up and overwhelm them with their votes for the person with the best haircut.

An Unignorant Candidate

Imagine a candidate for office who was incredibly intelligent. One who quoted Shakespeare in his speeches. One who could speak six languages without an accent. One who did theoretical physics in his spare time the way you or I do crossword puzzles, word searches, or differential calculus.

Picture the interview with him in his own home, his loaded bookshelves stretching off behind him, overflowing with tomes he was entirely familiar with and could expound on at length.

Try to imagine the three- and four-syllable words woven seamlessly into his speech, describing abstract concepts with perfect clarity, his mind showing a loose, dexterous, and flexible command of the problems his constituency faced.

Would he get elected? Not a chance in hell! Who would trust such a freak? Who wouldn't feel threatened by him and do everything they could to keep him and anyone like him as far from the controls as possible?

Power Ignored

Democracy is the power of the ignorant, make no mistake. But it trips itself up. How? Because so few people who are able to vote, bother to.

The genuinely ignorant don't know when there's an election happening. The partially ignorant don't know where their nearest voting station is. And the somewhat ignorant can't be bothered.

So, unfortunately, this power of the ignorant is unused. It's still the educated, wealthy, well-positioned, and informed elite who cast all the votes, and look at the result: a whole bunch of smartypantses in office, talking about things none of us can understand or care about anyway. Phooey!

Someday

Maybe someday, some distant, golden day, the ignorant hordes will rise and elect not just someone slightly substandard, but someone truly and genuinely stupid. Someone of such staggering ignorance that it's impossible to ignore. And those happy people will re-elect him.

A Box Of Books

I'd now like to ask you a few "rhetorical" questions, for which—and I cannot stress this enough—no verbal answers are needed.

1. How many rivers in Portugal begin with the letter "C"?

2. What's the Sanskrit word for "bashful"?

3. Where does "leather" come from?

You don't know, do you?

No one does.

We could spend years trying to find the answers to these and literally hundreds of questions just like them, and we'd wind up with nothing but a few dozen answers.

Key

The real key to being absolutely ignorant, is to rid yourself of all knowledge, and the first step to doing that, is to acknowledge that knowledge is bad.

This "lacknowledgement" is easier than you think. We all know that a little knowledge is a dangerous thing, so obviously a lot of knowledge would be even more dangerous.

We all know how annoying a smarty-pants is. Picture someone who knows ten times as much as a smarty-pants. Doesn't it naturally follow that they're ten times as aggravating?

Anchor

Think of how heavy books are to carry. Have you ever lugged a box of books? It's like a cardboard anchor. Imagine if that box of books was glued to your hands and you could never put them down. What a stiff back you'd have! What trouble you'd have eating! How peeved you'd get, always looking at that same box of books, everywhere you went. Well that's what it's like when you're carrying those books around *in your mind*. And think of how wet those books would get in your mind, given that the brain's over ninety percent water! And a wet book is an even heavier book.

Chapter 11
What You Don't Know Can't Hurt You

Imagine

Imagine you're sitting at home, reading a book.

I realize some of you may actually be at home, reading a book, in which case, this should be an easy enough thing for you to do. Those of you not at home will have to get your imaginations working a little harder of course, as will those of you who *are* at home but are not reading a book. If you're not currently at home *or* reading a book I would recommend coming back to this section when at least one of those applies to you.

For The Rest Of You

For the rest of you . . .

Imagine you're sitting at home, reading a book. Suddenly the door bursts open and a man comes in, holding a gun. He puts the gun against your head and says:

"Tell me right now, without looking in an encyclopedia, the name of the third president of Ghana. You have ten seconds."

The man begins to count.

"Ten.
"Nine.
"Eight.
"Seven.
"Six.
"Five.
"Four.
"Three.
"Two.
"One.
"Time's up! What's your answer?"

You shake your head, desperately trying to remember if the name that he's looking for has recently come up in conversation or during a trivia game. Finally you give up.

"I have no idea!" You say.

"Good." says the man, taking the gun away and stuffing it in the top of his pants. "If there's one thing I hate, it's a smarty-pants. If you had known the answer, I would have stabbed you, but now, I won't."

Woo

Now to you, the scenario I've just described probably seems like a fairy tale told to woo an over-thoughtful child to sleep, but it's not.

In fact, it's only one of literally nineteen very real situations in which ignorance could actually save your life.

Shield

Sometimes our ignorance can be like a shield that protects us in many different ways. In the example above we can see that ignorance can actually save our lives, but it can also spare us from physical pain.

Characters in movies often don't realize they've been shot until they look down and see the spreading bloodstain. Cartoon characters will often run off the edge of a cliff and not fall until they become aware that the ground is no longer beneath them.

Who's to say what would have happened if they had kept their ignorance intact? Perhaps even now they would be leading happy, fulfilled cartoon lives.

Left Arm

But ignorance doesn't just help fictional characters. I myself, Vaguen, have been spared incredible pain by ignorance.

When I was just twelve years old I broke my left arm playing soccer. A few days later my mother reluctantly took me to the hospital, where the doctor had to re-set the bone before applying the cast.

She told me it would be less painful if I didn't see what she was doing, so I didn't look. And I felt no pain at all—none.

It was my ignorance, combined with the morphine, that somehow saved me from excruciating agony.

Appendectomy

A man I once knew had had an appendectomy. The next day he found himself unable to urinate and in a great deal of discomfort.

He called the nurses and they brought a catheter. To the man's shocked eyes it looked like it was the width of a large man's thumb. He refused to let them bring it near him. They patiently told him it was the very one they'd used on him the day before when he was out cold. The man promptly lost consciousness. They inserted it, his problem was taken care of, and they removed it.

The next day he found the same difficulty, the nurses were called back, and the man passed out again. The routine was continued until his functions returned of their own accord. Yet he sustained no lasting physical injury.

In a state of ignorance the simple insertion of a catheter caused him no harm. It was only his conscious mind that rebelled.

Or did it? Perhaps his conscious mind knew enough to hand the man over to his own inner ignorance. Perhaps not. But perhaps.

Smoking

Consider how few people died from smoking before it was ever deemed a health risk: none.

Fear ... Of Bees!

John Cornelius, of Hoover, Quebec, attended one of my seminars and told me about his younger brother, who was terribly afraid of bees.

In a childhood game of Hide & Seek he'd stepped on a nest and been stung twenty-seven times, and had been unreasonably afraid of them ever since. The truly unfortunate thing was that he was a passionate gardener and there was simply no avoiding them.

Tired of running inside every time his eye caught anything that might be mistaken for a bee, he engaged the very costly services of a hypnotherapist. She worked with him for six months, at the end of which he emerged without even the slightest bit of knowledge that bees were any more dangerous than mosquitoes or houseflies.

Overcome!

From that day forward, whenever a bee came near him, he swatted it, and naturally, it stung him. But not being poisoned with the fear our culture injects in us that these tiny creatures are vicious killers, he felt no pain at all.

So what if his arms and face regularly puffed up to two or three times their normal size? Even the puffedupness didn't bother him, because he was too busy pretending to be a dog.

Nonchalant Reactions

This same insouciance can be witnessed in the nonchalant reactions to bees elicited by animals. Animals aren't so overcome by the knowledge of what could happen if they're stung that they overreact.

Have you ever seen a dog or a cat leap in terror and run from the room, screaming "Help! A bee! There's a bee on the window!"

We can see an even stronger reaction when people are confronted with spiders. They don't even hurt you. Except poisonous ones, or big ones, or the one that's behind you RIGHT NOW!

No, no, there's no spider there. But you were afraid for a second weren't you? THERE IT IS RIGHT THERE!

Just kidding of course. How could I po— THIS TIME I'M NOT JOKING! THERE REALLY IS ONE RIGHT BEHIND YOU!

Now, I'm sure you're getting pretty tired from the emotional roller-coaster ride I've just pushed you onto. And the rational part of your mind is trying to regain control, saying "How could he know? He's just a book!"

I can't deny that. I am just a book, so of course I can't really tell if there's a spider behind you, but does that mean there isn't?

And now that I've made you *think* of the possibility how relaxed can you really be when the normal sensations of your clothes rubbing against your skin feel like the crawling of tiny hairy legs. How sure are you that you don't hear the pitter-patter of eight feet behind you—or closer—or that you really are just randomly itching and there is no spider laying its eggs in your ear!

Once An Idea

Once an idea has been placed in your mind it can be difficult to shake off, and have very harmful consequences.

THERE'S THE SPIDER AGAIN!

As a child, my parents would often send me out into the world with the advice, "Make sure you're wearing clean underwear, young man. You could get hit by a bus and we'd look bad."

I have heard plenty of people who were given the same advice as a child, but in my mind the seed of healthy fear at the possibility of being run over by a bus grew into a tree of terror. (At the possibility of being run over by a bus.)

Obsessed

I became obsessed with the idea that I would be hit by a bus. Buses loomed in my imagination like wheeled nightmares. The fear soon overcame my conscious brain to the extent that I began to imagine that the buses that passed me would actually swerve in an attempt to run me down.

I saw buses everywhere! I took to walking to school across the fields but sometimes I would see a bus driving straight for me, miles from any road!

My imagination got the better of me time and again, and I was never brave enough to heed my parent's advice to just stand my ground and reveal these hallucinations for what they were.

It became so bad that I would grow terrified at anything that was associated with buses, and every morning as I answered my loving father's detailed questions about exactly where I would be walking that day my words would have to be forced out through the fear with which my heart filled at seeing his bus-driver's uniform.

?

Let Me Tell You

Let me tell you about an experiment done on a group of one hundred volunteers at Dalhousie University in Halifax, NS.

All hundred had 1000 ml of water dabbed onto their tongues with an eye-dropper. Fifty of them were told that their water contained the common cold virus. The other fifty were told theirs was distilled water.

After a week, they all reported back for an interview. The fifty who'd been told they'd been given a cold felt sick—every single one of them. They were sick, sneezing and coughing. Their eyelids drooped. The ones who'd been given distilled water felt fine.

But here's the interesting part—all *hundred* had been given distilled water. And nothing else.

The fifty who'd developed a cold hadn't received any virus from the water they'd been given. But they "knew" they'd been given an infection, and so they got sick.

Those fifty students were then given pills containing "sinus relief medicine" and a week later they reported back all saying they felt better. But what they'd really been given was corn starch!

Dead Hypochondriacs

There are many documented cases of hypochondriacs who have died simply because they believed they were terminally ill. After extensive autopsies were performed, nothing was found the matter with them—*not a single thing*—and they were declared dead.

Very similarly, there have been countless cases of people who have contracted deadly diseases, been unaware of it, and had those diseases knocked into oblivion by their immune systems. If they'd been diagnosed, they'd have despaired and fallen sick.

This can't be proven, of course, because the people it happened to were entirely unaware of it, told no one and are still unaware of it.

You might be one of those people. Have you ever had a mysterious pain in a finger, or in one ear that came and then went away? It might very well have been an illness others have died from because they merely thought they had it.

In-Depth Description

Have you ever heard someone give an in-depth description of an injury, and felt uncomfortable yourself—even though nothing physical was being done to you?

Have the pictures conjured in your mind ever caused you to swoon and faint—perhaps even throw up? Maybe you've seen photographs of bloody dismemberment and experienced the same thing. I know I have! Every time! I don't know why I keep looking at them!

Remember how tasty veal used to be before you knew where it came from? Or hot dogs, before you saw the people who prepared them? Or what about peaches? I still remember when my mother told me the truth about peaches. I didn't sleep for a week, just thinking about those poor, poor children. Every noise I heard I imagined to be the child-catchers coming to get me and carry me away to the peach-mines.

?

Madness

Often when people refer to an insane person, they say that that person has *lost his mind*.

This is not the time to look at how quickly these judgments tend to be made, I mean, I've seen people accused of insanity whose behaviour is no more unusual than the average university student's!

I would like to look at the assumption inherent in the phrase, "to lose one's mind." Which when you think about it is very misleading.

Watch An Insane Person

Watch an insane person on a bus or train. Pay particular attention to how they deal with their imaginary conversation partners. (Do this discreetly though, if you value your life!)

Crazy people talk to people they *know* are there. It's their very certainty that shows their insanity. You or I, approached by someone we weren't 100 percent sure was real, would speak to them very cautiously, dipping a toe into the possibility of their existence before taking the full plunge.

Sometimes

But it's not just the certainty of the *presence* of people that shows insanity. Concrete knowledge of the fact that *no one's* there—when there quite clearly is someone—is another indicator.

I discovered recently that a friend of mine had this exact problem. He adamantly clung to his knowledge that my mother was not in the room with us—which wasn't helped by her playing along and refusing to acknowledge him or touch him to prove that she was there! She just kept shaking her head at me, calling me a clever boy.

Dream Interpretation Through Ignorance

We should revel in our nightly excursions into deep states of ignorance. We should sleep as much as we can. All day, ideally. Dreams tell us things. And not many people have the tools to understand them, but fortunately I do.

Many deny dream interpretation has any validity. My dreams don't make sense, they say. Exactly. They're not supposed to. When we dream we use the real part of our minds—the part that laughs at what we call "making sense," and goes its own way entirely. And that part of the mind subscribes to the Power of Ignorance.

I have helped many people decipher their dreams. In a few cases, the interpretation sessions were recorded, and later someone sent me the tapes. Here are a few excerpts.

Excerpt #1:

(the following session involved a short man)

Short Man: I had this really weird dream last night.

(there is a pause)

Vaguen: Are you going to tell me about it?

Short Man: Oh—sure. Well, I was on this boat—this really small boat—and the water was all rough. The boat was rocking up and down, and I was getting seasick.

Then I noticed the boat was a lot bigger than it looked and there was a door and I went inside and there was this party going on. But the people had these big ears, and scaly eyes. There were plates of food, but it was all like, grass or something.

My brother was there, and Mark—this guy I used to work with. And they were doing that thing where one person locks their hands together with their fingers and the other person steps up into it and does a backflip and lands on their feet. But when my brother did it he crashed into a big ice sculpture of . . . of a beard, I think, but that doesn't make any sense.

Then I went out the door and I was on a street. I don't know what happened to the ocean. A taxi pulled up and the driver wanted me to get in but my brother was there and he grabbed my arm and said "don't get in."

Then I woke up.

Vaguen: I see. Let's start at the beginning.

> Now when you were on the boat and feeling seasick, you should have leaned over the side and vomited. You would have felt much better.
>
> And then, going inside to the party, you described the people as having big ears and scaly eyes and being served plates of grass. They were clearly reptiles. So it should have been a zoo you were going to, and not a party.
>
> This backflip your brother did crashing into the ice sculpture would have been much more satisfying if he'd landed on his feet and done a "ta-daa" pose. And you're right—it probably wasn't a sculpture of a beard. Perhaps of an animal, or a famous person. Certainly not a beard.
>
> And then emerging from the boat onto a street—you can't do that. You should have had the boat dock, and then walked onto the street.
>
> And the taxi—you should have gotten into it. Then we would have found out where it went, and maybe that would have been a better ending.
>
> (the short man is silent)

Excerpt #2:

(the following session involved a freckled woman)

Freckled Woman: Would you mind if I told you about the dream I had last night?

Vaguen: No

Freckled Woman: Well there was this house, but I couldn't get in. So I started peeling it like it was an orange. And I could tell there were these children inside trying to get out. So I started ripping harder and harder and when I finally got past the pulp the children were—

Vaguen: If you think that's bad, listen to this.

> I dreamed I was running from a bulldozer with a big face on the front of it, and it could follow me around corners and up stairwells and through doors. There was just no getting rid of it. And then finally it caught me and crushed me in its jaws and

mashed me into a paste and I was screaming "no! no! no!" and that's when I woke up.

But this other time I dreamed I was being chased by a big blue zipper that kept opening and closing itself and I was trying to get away by running on electric power lines, and the birds kept flying up and pecking at my eyes and I couldn't fight them off and finally I fell and I landed on my head, and that's when I woke up.

And then another time I dreamed I was eating a great big peach.

Now those are weird dreams. Wouldn't you agree?

(the freckled woman is silent)

Excerpt #3:

(the following session involved a bald man)

Bald Man: This is the dream I've been having every night since my wife's relatives have been staying with us.

Vaguen: (says nothing)

Bald Man: I'm in the living room, and my wife and her mother and her uncle and his girlfriend and her kids tell me they'd like to do something special for me. I say okay, and they wrap a warm towel around my head. And then I can feel them doing something but I can't tell what it is. Then they unwrap the towel and I look down and they've taken off all my clothes. And I'm covered in leeches. Hundreds of them. All over my body, and I know they're sucking me dry. And I've been castrated. And they're all laughing.

Vaguen: What then?

Bald Man: That's all there is. I just lie there, bleeding. Usually I can see one of them has taken my wallet. Then I wake up.

Vaguen: Hmmm.

   (a long pause ensues)

Vaguen: I have no idea what this dream means.

   (the bald man is silent)

   (end of excerpts)

   If you'd like to tell me any of your dreams, I'd be glad to help you as I've helped the people above. Think of a dream you've had recently. Think of as much detail as you can remember. Good. Now tell it to me.

Of course, I won't be able to hear you.

Perhaps you'd be better off telling it to a living human being.

Or just take one of the interpretations cited above. I'm sure it'll apply.

I'm happy to have helped you.

Chapter 11
Declare Bankruptcy Of The Mind

Forget Everything

One of the greatest sources of unhappiness in most people's lives is missed opportunities.

"If I had *known* he was going to offer me a promotion" they'll say "I never would have thrown my coffee in his face" or "It *seemed* like any other day, so I just didn't bother dressing up" or "If only I'd *known* there was a pencil lodged in the wall just there!"

Often these people will cite these as examples of times when ignorance didn't help them. They may even blame ignorance for losing their jobs, marriages, or hearing!

But it wasn't a lack of knowledge that tripped these people up, so much as *too much knowledge*—or you might say—a lack of *ignorance*.

Normal People

Most normal people, when they wake up in the morning, if asked, could give you a pretty detailed description of the day before. And this is reasonable.

Where we begin to see worrying signs of over-knowledgement is when these people are asked to describe the day that they are about to have. They will be able to tell you about their breakfast, their trip to work, their day at work—including lunch, their trip home (stopping for a donut) and their evening, including what they're having for dinner—all things that haven't happened yet.

They "know" exactly what will happen each moment of the day, and it is this "knowledge" that causes the problems listed a few paragraphs ago.

Dangerous Surprises

The world is a huge complicated place, one that more often than not holds dangerous surprises. But ignorance allows us to go through each day with no surprises. Because what is a surprise but something unexpected? And what is expectation, but *knowledge* of something that will happen?

You will be far less likely to have expectations about any day if you begin it ignorantly, with the words "I don't know what's going to happen today! It could be anything! Hello! Who are you?" than if you wake up and say, "Aaaaargh! Who the hell are you and what are you doing in my bedroom? No I'm not going to describe what happened yesterday! I'm gonna kick your ass!"

Embrace It

An ignorant man, faced with something unexpected, will embrace it as an opportunity, diving headlong into the experience and seeing where it takes him. Whereas a man who expects his life to follow a certain routine will see the unexpected as a threat and resist it, futile though that may be.

Imagine how earth-shattering it would be to the man with expectations if the planet on which we live were to suddenly break into millions of pieces! But the ignorant man would take it in his stride, embracing it as another in a series of wonderfully unexpected turns of events.

Which one do you think is happier?

Where The Hell Are My Damn Keys?!

Imagine that you can't find your keys. You know they're in the house somewhere. First you check all the obvious places; the pants you were wearing last night, your purse, that little table that you keep meaning to get into the habit of putting them on.

Then, when you've exhausted the more obvious places you'll start to go for those less likely spots; under the cushions of your couch, on top of the TV with your remote or in the cutlery drawer with your cutlery.

At this point someone might helpfully say, "Have you tried looking in the car?" to which you'll respond, "I know they won't be in there!!!"

Eventually you find them, sitting on the dashboard of—you guessed it—your car.

What?

What is this phenomenon? It's a clinging to only one area of ignorance: "I admit I don't know where they *are*" and it's a denial of another area: "but I won't admit I don't know where they *aren't*."

Now, on the slim chance that you understand what I'm talking about (and I often don't!) you're probably wondering how to apply this lesson to other areas in your life. Don't. It really only covers finding small things that you've lost, like keys.

?

Back In Time Again

Now imagine that you went back in time again. You might run into yourself. "Stop teasing those people!" you'd say.

Let's say you continued plummeting backwards in time until you'd reached two hundred years into the past.

If you were to speak to the primitive peoples you found there you'd find that they "knew" a lot of things that we now know aren't true.

Imagine if you tried to explain to them that the earth wasn't flat, but spherical, or that the sun wasn't some kind of magical fiery chariot that was ridden across the sky each day by a guy in a hat, but was in fact a burning ball of gas that circled the earth once every twenty-four hours.

They would treat you as if you were crazy, although you would be right.

Perhaps there are a lot of times when people are treated as insane when they're not. Hmmmm? Yes.

The point is everything we think we know is subject to change, so our grip on what we perceive as reality should be a loose one at best.

Open Mind

To sum up.

We all know the value of an open mind. If a mind is truly open it must be like an unfenced field, with no walls to keep knowledge in, no burly guards to grab knowledge as it tries to wander away for a brief visit home, leading it back to its room, holding its arm much too tightly, smiling a smile that never reaches their eyes.

?

Job Market

Look at this! Another letter!

> I was a top executive at a national company's Midwest headquarters in Muncie, Indiana when some personal difficulties required that I leave the position I held and put my career on hold for a while.
> Two years ago things had settled down for me and it was time to "get back on the saddle."
> I needed a job, but since I hadn't been in the job-market for some time I was a little worried that employers would immediately discard my resume in favour of someone with more recent experience.

Stand Out

> I heard about a position that had become available and I knew there would be a lot of competition. I decided to give myself an edge with my application, and in the middle of the night came up with an idea to make my resume stand out.
> This company was known mostly for its competitively priced fast food, so my first step was to obtain one of the wrappers they put take-out food in. I printed my resume on *this*, with the information arranged in the style of their menu, offering several

different "combos" of my skills. In my cover letter I paraphrased their commercials, offering everything I had with "special sauce." My final touch was to learn my resume by heart, and practise saying it very quickly until I could recite the whole thing in less than a minute.

Flying In The Face Of Discouragement

Everyone I spoke to *knew* that my approach was wrong.

"That's just not how it's done!" they told me.

But I decided that I didn't *know* this.

And I got the job.

I used my ignorance every day when I served the customers and came very close to being Employee Of The Month twice.

In the two years since I re-entered the job-market I've used my new strategy successfully forty times. Giving my application form inside a pizza box for a pizza delivery position, and organizing my resume into "aisles" to be a stock-boy at a major drug-store chain. I'll always be glad that I don't *know* how these things are done!

Very glad indeed!

?

Wrong Conclusions

Let's look at another way knowledge can steer us wrong.

A red-haired man once approached me after one of my seminars and told me the following story:

Automobile

He'd been having trouble with his automobile. It was making a "funny" noise. The man admitted that he was no expert, but he could tell the noise came from the engine.

As many car owners do, he ignored the noise.

The noise, unfortunately, persisted. Several days later, the noise having grown in volume, he pulled over to the side of the road and propped open the hood.

He stared at the strange instruments he found in there, and eventually noticed the radiator's cap was slightly loose. Protecting his hand from its heat with his tie, the man reached to tighten the cap, but the instant before he touched it, something very curious happened: the noise stopped.

Silence

The man's hand retreated. He stared at the engine, now enveloped in unfamiliar silence. He waited for three minutes, but the noise didn't resume.

He returned to the driver's seat, started the engine, and drove off in peace and quietude.

He smiled to himself, thinking that if he'd moved only a little faster, he would have tightened that cap, and the noise would have simultaneously stopped entirely of its own accord. And it would have had nothing to do with him. Yet he would have "known" that it had. But he would have known falsely. And he would have boasted of his actually empty accomplishment to everyone he knew.

Leave It Alone

From that day forth, the man told this story to all his friends and business connections. Advising them to "Leave it alone. Your engine knows what it's doing. Give it the time it needs to work out its own kinks."

He lost a lot of friends this way, but consoled himself with the success of his scrap metal business.

?

Pills

In any complex system it's difficult to know exactly what

cause brings about what effect.

After one of my seminars I was approached by a man who seemed very excited. We chatted for a while and he sent me this letter.

I should warn you: he comes from jolly old England. To be honest I didn't understand most of what he said or wrote, but he was just so cute to listen to. Hopefully his letter is relevant to the topic we're discussing right now.

Limey Letter

To whom it may concern,
 I have had, I *must* say, a lot of trouble sleeping ever since I was involved in a *little jaunt* into the woods of *Maine*, that's stateside don't you know.

You see I was staying at the newly-bought *lodge* of some chums of mine. They'd snapped it up for a song after the property had been empty for *donkey's years*. Some terrible scandal I'd heard.

My chums obviously realized that my presence at the opening of their little inn gave the place some much needed *grandeur*, and were letting me stay there *gratis*.

Stiff Upper

I was using the time to recover the old *stiff upper* after a bit of a *rum* pass further south. I'd been involved in some local *argy-bargy*, practically had a bridge fall on my head, you see.

But to cut a long story short, there I was, taking a woodland *constitutional* and worrying about those *damn bears* when I stumbled on what looked initially like a huge bird's nest. On closer inspection the cloth scraps I'd seen turned out to be the clothing still being worn by twelve human corpses.

I must say I did the *technicolour yawn* right away and nearly fainted. I hadn't seen anything quite so horrific since university, when I'd watched as a good friend was pulped by a runaway robot during some experiment with some *science johnnies*.

Good And Proper

Needless to say, the shock did me in *good and proper*, and I spent the next two years having nightmares. I'd wake up screaming, trying to rid myself of the memory of that one particularly tall corpse whose arm, strangely capable-looking even though it was half-eaten by creepy-crawlies, pointing exactly away from the lodge that was fifty feet behind him.

I was well on the way to ending up *stark-staring mad* when some heaven-sent angel of mercy in a doctor's outfit finally gave me some pills.

Tickety-boo and they did the trick. A few years later and there I was, nightmare free, sanity restored but popping pills every *bally* night.

Now, where I come from, we don't take lightly to chemical addiction and I knew that I had a monkey on the old back the size of Mighty Joe Young.

Well, this one night I was right on the verge of taking my pills when I decided enough was enough. With Heraclean effort I put down my glass of water and let the pills fall onto my bedside table. Terrified, I went to sleep.

Trousers

I woke up screaming, my nightmare still fresh in my mind. Those eleven small corpses and the one larger one, his long femurs showing through the holes in his half-eaten trousers.

I decided to put off my cold turkey until another night so I grabbed the pills from my night-table and knocked them back. I slept like the proverbial log.

"Well," said I upon waking, "It looks like I'll be stuck with these pills for some time."

But when I looked, the pills were still right there on

the table. What wasn't there was a pile of buttons that I'd left out to sew onto my pyjamas.

So, the pills didn't stop my nightmares at all, but if this hadn't happened, I would never have known that. I would have still "known" that pills stop nightmares, and I would never have discovered the spiritual healing power of magic pyjama-buttons.

There Are Great Disadvantages to Knowledge

There are great disadvantages to knowledge.

A man who'd attended one my seminars told me about a company dinner he'd attended three years before. His boss had been regaling the assorted guests with a lively tale that hinged on the quotation "The fool doth think he is wise, but a wise man knows himself to be a fool" which he credited as being from the Bible. At this point, one of the guests—a thin man with spectacles—cleared his throat very loudly and kept doing so until all eyes were on him. There was a frightening silence.

The man said, "I'm sorry to correct you, boss, but that's a quote from Shakespeare."

"Nonsense!" said the boss. "Do you think I don't know my Bible inside and out?"

"I'm afraid you don't, because that line is from *As You Like It*, by William Shakespeare."

"Horseshit!" declared the boss, and stormed off to the bookshelf. He drew out a large volume of the *Complete Works of Shakespeare* and a *King James Bible*. He flipped open the Bible and said "Now lemme see here ... it's in the book of Kings, I think, or maybe Kings 2 ... now wait just a minute ... goddam pages keep sticking together ... well now where was it, I was just thinking about it the other day."

The thin guest, in the meantime, opened the thick compendium of Shakespeare and soon found the exact page on which that very quote lay. He ostentatiously cleared his throat once more, and read the quote off the page. He then paraded the book around and presented it to as many of the embarrassed guests as he could induce to read it.

Lost Status

Needless to say, this man soon lost his status as a favourite of the boss, and the very next year received a mild reprimand for keeping an untidy desk (although everyone knew what the real reason was!), and a much less impressive raise than he'd boasted he'd get.

Let's See What Would Have Happened

But let's see What Would Have Happened If This Man Had Chosen Ignorance. Or acronymically ... WWHHICHI!).

On hearing the boss's story, he wouldn't have recognized the quote at all, and would never have challenged his boss's crediting it as being from the Bible.

In fact, he wouldn't have read the Bible, or even heard of such an obscure volume of esoteric mythology, so how would he have had a literary standard to trace the source? He wouldn't have, any more than if the boss had said it was from the Upanishads, the Epic of Gilgamesh, or the Teutonic legends that formed the inspiration for Wagner's Ring Cycle.

Given that the quote was in fancy-pants "olde style Englishe", he wouldn't have understood it all, and would have resorted to smiling and nodding until the boss got back to speaking properly. The boss would have looked on his audience and been immediately drawn to the thin man's receptive smiling, bobbing face and felt good that his story had been so well received. He would have beamed with the warmth of the feeling that he was loved by those subordinate to him.

The thin man never would have received that dreadful reprimand, and would have been so surprised to get any raise in pay at all the following year that he would have toppled over with delight and gratitude.

Now that sounds like a man who's going somewhere! Straight to the top! That's right, Ignorance is a one way ticket to the CEO's office. And not just for a scolding!

Not Just Not Knowing Things

But what if the man had accidentally known the quote was incorrectly attributed? What then? Huh?

Well there's still no reason why he couldn't have chosen Ignorance. Ignorance isn't just not knowing things, it's choosing to ignore what you know.

It wouldn't have taken that much mental agility to consider the possibility that perhaps his own knowledge of literary and Bible-things was faulty, and that the boss was right. Given that the first performance of *As You Like It* predates the publication of the *King James Bible* by seven years, he could have assumed the quote appeared in both texts, perhaps one in reference to the other. It's possible Shakespeare himself inserted it into the Bible working under a pseudonym, subtly quoting himself as a clever reference to his own work and thus leaving a calling card to the ages, the way many Shakespearean scholars postulate he inserted his own name—broken in half—into the 44th psalm.

But even if these academic arguments still grated with the man's sense of truth, he could have sat there, repeating the Igmantra as loud and as long as he needed to until the episode was long past and the conversation had moved on to other things.

Take Your Cue From the Ostrich

But what if even the Igmantra wasn't enough!! In situations like these (and in other situations too), we need to take our cue from the ostrich, the paragon of the animals.

The Bible (or it might be Shakespeare!) tells us that when we give to charity, our right hand shouldn't know what our left is doing. These are sound words. The finest demonstration of this kind of behaviour is practised by the ostrich, which will periodically stick its hand in a hole in the ground. With one hand deep in a hole, the other hand has no idea what it's doing, and it can practise all the charity it wants. What a noble creature! What an example for us all!

Imagine yourself at that dinner party, silencing the alarms in your mind as a quote is dreadfully misattributed, by doing nothing other than finding a hole somewhere on the floor, and plunging your hand into it for as long as it took the boss to move on to another story.

Like Rats Steering a Sinking Ship

Another disadvantage to knowledge is the extreme inflexibility it breeds. Someone who "knows" they have the right answer will rarely back down, even if presented with solid evidence to the contrary, like a book. The boss in the above story went to his grave swearing the quote was from the Bible, and had it chiselled on his tombstone, attributed as such—engendering more than few titters from the mourners at his burial, let me tell you!

But what if that piece of knowledge had been more than a simple disagreement on fiction? What if he'd been the captain of a ship and refused to acknowledge that his navigational calculations were steering the ship in large figure eights? What if he'd "known" that icebergs are soft, crumbly and entirely visible from the surface of the water? What if he'd insisted that he knew where he was and would be able to pilot the ship into a safe port in the Azores hours before the jagged holes in the ship's hull caused the thing to plunge to the ocean floor? What would have happened to him? He would have died gurgling, and the world would be glad to be rid of such a stubborn smarty-pants, that's what.

Whereas a captain who was open and flexible (read: IGNORANT) and didn't insist he knew everything at all times would have heeded the warnings of his crew and his own queasy stomach and stopped steering in wild, crazy eights. He would have stayed clear of the icebergs, fearful of the crap movie he'd inspire years later if he hit one. And as the ship sunk, he'd have had no idea where he was and run screaming and crying like a little girl, burying himself under a blanket on the nearest lifeboat, and eventually made it to shore to sire legions of likeminded spawn. Once again, witness the triumphant Power of Ignorance!

Chapter 13
Knowledge Is Impossible

The Most Popular Letter In the Alphabet

What's the most interesting thing to anyone? Easy. Themselves. A study undertaken by the New York City Telephone Enthusiasts Society sought out which is the most popular letter of the alphabet (which doubles as an entire word) used by callers whilst speaking in the first person. Over nine thousand calls were secretly monitored.

The winner: "I."

People love talking about themselves. They love thinking about themselves, hearing about themselves, feeding themselves, dressing themselves, shaving themselves. And when someone looks in a mirror, what part of their reflection draws their eye first?

You guessed it: themselves.

The Illusion of Ourselves

And yet how well do we know ourselves? Here's an exercise:

List what you did (specifically) and with whom you did it for each of the last sixteen New Year's Eves. You have thirty seconds.

Time's Up

Time's up.

It's difficult, isn't it?
Now here's one that's even harder:
What did you have for lunch four Wednesdays ago?

Here are some more:

Which pair of socks did you wear April 12th, 1989?

How many veins do you have?

What was your least favourite gift on your eighth birthday?

On which date last January did you clip your fingernails for the first time?

What was the third most exciting moment of your twenty-second summer?

How many showers have you taken?

What's your library card number (don't look!)?

What's your earliest memory of the word "corn"?

What were you doing the day Saul Bellow died?

You don't know the answers to these questions, do you. Even though they're on your favourite subject. Just how much do you really know about yourself?

The Warping of Memory

Here's another exercise: Name three movies you remember having loved as a child or teenager, but haven't seen since then. Now go out and rent them.

Weren't they awful? Didn't you recognize certain elements from your memory of those movies, but weren't they somehow badified?

How is it that your memory didn't warn you that the movie would be so dated, with corny special effects, false settings, and obvious jokes?

If you want an even greater shock see which of your favourite childhood TV shows are available on DVD. Don't buy them, trust me. Rent them. You may need a bottle of whiskey to get you through this one.

Fallacy

So how much is it even possible to know about anything when we know so little about our favourite subject? Isn't the very idea of knowledge simply a great big towering fallacy?

?

You Forget Instantly

Most people don't read. But even those who do don't actually pay attention to what they're reading. And even those who pay rapt attention quickly forget most of what they've read anyway.

How good is the average person's memory? How much can you recall from the books you read one, two, or even three years ago? Nothing. How clear is your picture of something you read just this afternoon (assuming you're reading this in the evening)? Or one page ago?

Simple Test

Try this simple test:

How many commas were there on the middle third of the preceding page?

Don't cheat.

The correct answer is "I don't know."

You see, even the greatest sage's memory is bound within certain limits. Much less yours. And as the above exercise demonstrated, you can't even remember the simple things. How would you have fared with a test on something more complex?
Not well my friend.
Not well at all.
Pretty badly indeed.

Where Is It?

But consider this: not too long ago you would have known the precise total of all the punctuation marks on that page. Where has that knowledge gone? It must be somewhere.

What Have You Done?

Have you ever been reminiscing with a friend, and at one point they mention an incident in which you were involved, but you have simply no recollection of it? And from the way they tell the story—in which a former version of yourself is a more than active participant—you can tell they're not making it up, and yet you still can't remember it for yourself.

Isn't that disconcerting?
It's nothing to be ashamed of!
We're all like that.

What happened to that former version of you that had those experiences? You certainly remembered them while they were happening. It wasn't until years later that you didn't realize that they'd disappeared from your mind.

Or had they?
No they hadn't.

Brain

There are vast portions of the human brain that are never used. A more than infinite chasm of almost bottomless depths exists within each of us, full of lost memories, missing details, and broken dreams. Broken, shriveled-up, trampled-on dreams.

This is where those old stories about us go. And discarded opinions. And memorized lines for our parts in Christmas concerts.

This is also where what we read goes. The gist of it remains—sometimes—but the words, sentences, and commas get thrown into the mental abyss.

Most of the words you've just been reading are already there.

That last sentence is well on its way.

You probably just glanced at it again. That won't help.

So why read at all, you may ask. Why indeed. If the book is going to end up in the cranial dumpster, why not just put there in the first place?

?

The Something-burg Uncertainty Principle

Science and ignorance are generally thought not to mix, but they do. Remember the uncertainty principle?

The uncertainty principle teaches us that there are limits to what it is possible to know.

Thanks to my Power of Ignorance, I was unable to remember the name of the uncertainty principle. I knew it was "something-burg," and was pretty sure it began with "H."

A Scientist Friend

I knew that a scientist friend of mine would be able to fill in the blanks for me, so I paid him a visit and asked him to explain the uncertainty principle to me.

"Let's say I have a cat." He began.

"OK." I replied, already bored.

"Now let's say that I've put this cat into a sealed lead container, to which I've attached a complicated system, whereby the release of one atom from a sample of throntignium will release a deadly poisonous gas into th—"

"You monster!" I cried, grabbing him by the lapels of his white lab-coat. "Where is it? Is it here? You've got to open that box right now!"

"No wait!" He squeaked. "You don't understand."

"Oh, I understand well enough! Living things are just toys to you and your god-like domain of science! When did you stop being human in the pursuit of knowledge? Now tell me where the cat is . . ." At this point I grabbed a glass beaker, smashed it on to the edge of a counter top and held the jagged shards against his squirming nerdy face. ". . . or you *don't want to know* what I'll do to you."

"There is no cat!" he managed to gasp.

I felt like I'd been kicked in the stomach. I looked down, but could see no evidence that I had been. What I was feeling was just the shock of reality, and a feeling of powerlessness and futility.

"So I'm already too late." I released my grip, and he slid away from me, backing up against the wall of the lab, his eyes darting, looking for a way out. I felt sick and weary.

"I'm going." I told him, "but if I ever hear about a cat going missing, if I ever see so much as one poster with people looking for their kitten, you'll wish you'd never told me your sick little secret."

Possible Life

I try not to think too much about that cat. I like to think that, because I've never found that container, and opened it, never seen the dead cat inside, in a way, it still exists in a state of possible life. It's not much, but that's all I can give it. That, and a name. I call him Purkey.

Lost Avenue

With this avenue of questioning lost to me, I turned to the Power of Ignorance to solve the problem of the name of the uncertainty principle. H——burg. Let's say it's the Hindenburg Uncertainty Principle. That would make sense. It could be explained like this.

Is it helium or hydrogen?
I don't know.
Light a match.
If it doesn't burn, it must be helium.

As mentioned earlier, the Hindenburg uncertainty principle teaches us that there are limits to what it is possible to know. That the act of trying to observe something, to know it, changes it.

Unless it's helium.

?

Science Equals Guesses

On those rare occasions when we normal people think of scientists, we think of them as people who know things.

But science is not the same as knowledge. All science is just a set of theories, which we could just as easily call guesses, that suit the facts.

We can tell science is not knowledge by the fact that scientific theories don't last. They exist for a while, then are disproven, and replaced with other theories. These too will then exist, be disproven and replaced, and so on.

Wrong

Hundreds and hundreds of years ago, *in the past*, scientific theories would last for hundreds and hundreds of years before this process of disproval took place.

Nowadays, theories will last just a few decades, perhaps even years.

And hundreds and hundreds of years from now, *in the future*, scientific theories will last only a few months, or weeks.

And as science progresses, scientific theories will be disproven faster and faster. Eventually within days, then hours.

Ignorance Helps

Scientists who have used the Power of Ignorance in their research have reached this advanced stage already.

Many of them have produced theories that have been disproven in record time—often within seconds—usually as soon as they show their work to another human being. Once by one of the very children they were experimenting on.

?

Physical Laws

It is only an illusion that the physical laws that prevent us from doing the impossible prevent us from doing the impossible.

Our belief in these laws is so strong that we give them power.

We came up with them and we perpetuate them.

We don't have to.

With ignorance we can overcome them. Not believing them is difficult. But it can be done.

Walls

Consider this: walls aren't actually solid. Current scientists assure us that matter consists of atoms that are composed almost entirely of empty space.

Even an atom in a brick wall is just a cloud of mostly empty space nestled amongst hundreds of other clouds of mostly empty space. Arranged in a brick wall pattern. A sort of brick wall of mostly empty space. That's all brick walls are. That's all we are. Or anything is.

Furthermore these brick walls only tend to exist. As do we and everything else.

Straight Through

When we were young, most of us were told by our parents that thunder was caused by clouds bumping into each other. Because the clouds were distracted by our constant questions and whining. And every time they bumped thunder happened and puppies died.

We stopped believing this story pretty early on in our adult lives. We know now that clouds would pass right through each other if they didn't look where they were going, with no harm done to either of them!

So why continue to believe that another kind of mostly empty cloud—a person—can't pass through a second mostly empty cloud—a brick wall.

An Unforgettable Demonstration

Many years ago I was explaining this to an audience in one of my seminars when I sensed they had reservations. They were shuffling their feet and there was more than the usual amount of hushed voices saying "Stuff and nonsense!"; "A load of superstitious mumbo-jumbo!" and "What price boobery!"

I decided right then that I had to "put my money where my mouth was" and give them a demonstration of just what can be achieved if you truly know nothing.

After just twenty minutes of musing I hatched a plan. I raced to the back of the stage, drew back the rear curtain and revealed a thick, sturdy brick wall.

I turned and looked at the audience, then back at the wall. I slapped it a few times to prove to myself and the audience that it was a real wall, and not a fake theatrical set. I took ten paces backwards, removed my jacket and gathered myself up into a posture of one preparing to run, very much like a runner at the starting line.

As what I was planning to do sank in I could hear their voices again. "He isn't is he?!"; "He is!" and "Oh no!"

Wiggled Eyebrows

I scuffed my right foot on the floor like an angry bull in an arena then looked back at the audience. As I wiggled my eyebrows I saw one very tall hirsute man turn to his friend.

"That old man's mad." He said in a conversational tone.

This was obviously the opinion of everyone in the room. They knew that I couldn't pass through the wall.

But I knew no such thing.

I smiled at them, angled my head down and ran as fast as I could straight at the wall.

Sting

I felt a very slight uncomfortable sting as I passed through the solid wall, and as I shivered in the chill of the night-time air I regretted taking off my jacket.

I'm sure I was as surprised as everyone else. I took a few seconds to appreciate the moment. I had achieved the impossible. I had used my Power of Ignorance and bypassed the laws of physics. I had run through a brick wall.

As solid as that wall was it couldn't keep out the noise of my audience suddenly bursting into a mysterious slapping sound. I could hear their cheering and whistles along with a slapping sound that I didn't recognize. I took a deep breath and tried not to smile too broadly as I trotted around to the front of the venue. Word had already spread and I had to fight my way through crowds of reporters and an astronaut just to get back inside. When I finally got back into the auditorium I realized that it was actually the gymnasium of my old school. And there were all the people I'd met in university!

Proud Parents

I was worried that getting to the stage would be difficult but the crowd lifted me onto their shoulders, gently passing me from one to the next. The stage was relinquished by a tall gangly man telling stories about an old job he'd once had, and a shorter man in a suit, who did a flip and landed flat on his back. When I got to the stage my parents were waiting for me. They were smiling and telling me how proud they were of me. Then my mother stepped aside and I saw that she had been standing in front of Fluffy, a puppy I'd owned as a child. I'd thought he was dead.

The cheering was still going on, and I looked out at the audience. I realized the slapping sound I'd been unable to recognize was coming from their hands. Everyone in the room was hitting their palms together quickly and repeatedly. It sounded wonderful.

Somehow, and I can't explain it, over this thunderous whooping and "clapping" I heard someone say my name very quietly.

I turned and saw a beautiful woman with long brown hair. She had a sad expression on her face and whispered in my ear.

"Enjoy this my love. But remember, one day you and I could be happy for real."

She turned and left but try as I might I couldn't follow her.

Headache

Finally I returned to the stage where my audience continued to cheer. I don't know how much time passed like this, but eventually their cheering began to give me quite a headache. I decided to take a nap until it went away. I went to the spot in the wall that I had run though, lay down on my back and stared at the bricks until I fell asleep.

When I woke up I was alone. The people had respectfully left and all the lights were off. My amazement at what I'd achieved flooded into me again, and if it hadn't been for my headache I might have convinced myself that it had never happened.

Ever Since

I have ended my seminars like this ever since. Often when I meet people who've attended they'll tell me it was the ending that really stuck with them.

"I can't believe you did that!" They'll say, laughing. And they'll show the love and care that my opening their minds has inspired by asking "How's your head?"

"Still got a bit of a headache." I'll reply, and we'll laugh. They'll usually stop laughing before I do.

Delusional Madman

Not everyone is capable of opening their minds to the new way of thinking my demonstration necessitates, and from time to time I meet people who've been so unable to cope that they have actually blocked out the memory of what they saw, substituting it with a delusion which better fits their concept of "reality."

I avoid these people, not because I don't like them, but because I respect their need for delusion. I'm sure it's the only way they can be happy, and why would I take that away from them?

A Christmas Tale

In 1956, a certain nine-year-old boy lay in a ward of a hospital in Sault Ste. Marie, Ontario. He was waiting for an operation on his kidneys. It was Christmas Day.

His family lived hours away and had been snowed in. Earlier a group of people dressed as clowns, musicians and Santa Clauses had gone from room to room, handing out presents and singing songs, but through an inexplicable mishap they'd missed him entirely.

Wasn't Pleased

The nurse on duty wasn't pleased with having to work that day, and told the little boy as much. She begrudgingly brought him a Christmas dinner with turkey, cranberry sauce, and mashed potatoes, but then took it away when she remembered his condition didn't allow him to eat solid food. She stepped on the foot pedal of the garbage can next to his bed and dumped the food in, giving him a good long look at it (and a good whiff) before she closed the lid. She threw down the tray with a loud metallic crash and announced the end of her shift, pulling on a coat and scampering off laughing.

A Miracle

The little boy felt his lower lip begin to quiver as his loneliness overcame him. Christmas was his favourite time of year. Wasn't this when miracles happened? Suddenly something caught his eye. There was someone at the door! He looked up ... no one. It had been a trick of the light.

He waited and waited, but no one came to visit him. No nurse, doctor, intern, orderly, or kindly other patient who was suffering worse than him but kept up an inspirationally brave front came in even to ask if he knew what time it was—no one at all.

The clock in the room ticked so loudly he couldn't sleep. The IV needle jammed in his arm was incredibly painful. From down the hall he could hear the distant celebrations of other patients whose families had braved the few inches of snow. He heard the carols they sang and the squeals of joy as they unwrapped their presents. With every yelp of mirth he was reminded of the good time he wasn't having. He lay there by himself, and wept until he lost consciousness.

That Night

That night, a doctor crept into his room and gently woke up him. The boy's eyes fluttered open.

"Young man," the doctor said "I'm afraid we still haven't found a suitable kidney donor. It looks like you're going to be in here for a very, very long time."

The doctor playfully thumped him on the back and left. The clicking of his heels on the hard hospital floor echoed as the doctor walked down the long, cold hallway.

The Point

That story is one of the countless tales of abject misery that are a grave and constant element of the human experience. But isn't life so much sunnier when you don't know about those things? Or at least don't know them in specific detail? Doesn't it make it hard to enjoy anything at all when you have an abundant knowledge?

Chapter 14
Don't Worry, Be Ignorant

The Shortcut

On April 12th, 1922, Franklin Singer decided to take a shortcut home from work. It was his daughter's eighth birthday, and he was excited to see her. The freight yard between his work and his home was fenced off for reasons of safety, but there were many gaps and holes made by hoboes. Franklin sneaked through one of them, ducked across the tracks without looking and was whammed by a speeding locomotive engine. He died instantly.

Later, when two freight yard attendants discovered his body, one remarked to the other "The poor bastard—he never knew what hit him."

A Better Death

We have a perception that it would have been a better death for Mr. Singer if he'd got his foot caught in the tracks and been able to watch that locomotive for ten minutes as it closed the distance and then conked him into the next life.

If that had happened, would anyone have said "that lucky duck—he got a great big, long look at what hit him"?

Mugged

Would you rather be mugged by an eight foot tall barbarian wielding a battleaxe, or have your pocket picked by a shadow?

You're Dumped

If someone were choosing to end a relationship with you, would you rather they stood in your apartment and told you why for hours and hours, listing all of your faults and their frustrations with you, and then rubbing salt in the wound by sending you letters about it, or would you rather they just left, at most leaving a tiny note saying they didn't want to see you again?

The Necessity of Ignorance

Life is full of unpleasantnesses. If we allowed ourselves to dwell on even half of the suffering and misery and poverty and wretchedness and cruelty and needless spite in the world, (not to mention the inequality, prejudice, malicious twists of fate, disfiguring turns of events, and incidents in which complete strangers spit in one's face) we'd surely go crazy.

Ignorance, viewed in this light, is a powerful coping mechanism. Nay—a necessity.

The Waitress Story

A woman who'd attended one of my seminars in Kingston, Ontario, cornered me and told me a long, dull, poorly-paced story about the restaurant where she worked as a line cook. Here are the heavily edited highlights. Severely edited.

Five years ago, one of her co-workers—Louise McKinnon—had given notice to her manager that New Year's Day would be her final day of work.

Mr. Stephens, her manager, was very distressed by her decision and didn't leave his office all morning. Louise was his best waitress and he knew it, but he'd never really told her.

Speech

At the end of the day he called a meeting of all of his employees and made a speech. He began by telling them that Louise had given him her notice. He went on to tell the story of how green she'd been when she applied for the job three years before, retelling her awkward fumblings as she learned to wait tables. Oh how many plates she'd dropped!

In loving detail he told how she gradually won over the staff and customers and had since become nothing less than the heart and soul of the restaurant. He told her she was someone none of them would ever forget, and—holding back tears—that they simply couldn't make it without her.

Shedding tears of joy Louise said she'd stay.

Huge Pay Raise

Stephens learned a valuable lesson that day, and he swore that he would always make every member of his staff feel appreciated.

He went home that night and told his wife what he'd done. He repeated the story at a conference of restaurateurs, and was recruited to the management team of a major chain, earning triple his previous wages.

And yet his material success was nothing compared to the warm glow he felt whenever he thought about Louise, and what a difference he'd made in her life. He slept soundly every night, with a broad smile on his face.

The Waitress Story Continues

At this point in her long ramble the woman deviated into a boring tangent, detailing the behind the scenes workings of the diner and the politics of wait-staff versus kitchen staff. For our purposes all we need to know is this . . .

Louise hadn't given any indication in her resignation letter of why she was leaving. The truth was that she'd accepted a marriage proposal. Her future husband had no qualms with her working, but it would have proven difficult for her to stay in Kingston, given that he lived in Hawaii. Knuckling under at Mr. Stephens's appeal, Louise tearfully broke off her engagement that night.

Louise is still at that same diner in Kingston. Her ex-fiancé found a new bride who now spends most of her time tanning.

Ashamed

Think of how ashamed Mr. Stephens would be if he knew the whole story! How much of the pleasure out of his own career rise would be leaked out like air from an old bicycle tire if he knew that it was all at the expense of a lonely waitress's one shot at happiness? He'd hardly be able to live with himself.

But he is. He feels just fine. He brags about what he did for her. Because he doesn't really *know* what he did for her.

At Last! The Conclusion

So how many disastrous incidents in your life would you rather know only up until a certain point, and be able to continue to see as triumphs with Disney endings?

?

Houdini

Harry Houdini was considered the greatest magician of his day. He gave over six thousand performances, and audiences were riveted by every one of them.

Once, after a particularly spectacular performance in Omaha, Nebraska, a reporter pounced on him in his dressing room and asked how he felt about the squealing crowd he'd just thrilled. Houdini turned very slowly, set down his bottle of whiskey and punched that reporter square in the face.

Some Guy You've Never Heard Of

Robert Llewellyn Maxwell was a stage actor who performed the role of King Lear a record one thousand and three times. How did he do it? How did he conjure up the magic to enrapture so many audiences for so long?

One young actor first saw him play the role in 1934, and it inspired him to go to acting school. He got his first paying job as a spear carrier in Maxwell's own production of King Lear. It was a dream come true. He quivered at the chance to study his idol from up close. With the stealthiness of a cat he shadowed Maxwell backstage and noticed that he always said what sounded like the same phrase right before he made an entrance. He sneaked close enough, undetected, to hear what Maxwell said. It was this: "Aw Christ, here we go again"

Some Woman

Celina Kidd was praised as the greatest acrobat the circus ever knew. Her stunts filled the tent everywhere she played. In Stoke-on-Trent, England, in 1924, it was advertised she'd do seven performances in a single day—more than double her normal load. Before the final performance, right before going on stage, she committed suicide. She left a note which said "If this only injures me, then for God's sake, someone finish the job."

What You Don't Know Can Entertain You

Consider the fact that a joke is funniest when you hear it for the first time. Imagine how boring it must be the hundredth time. Then consider the fact that many comedians milk the same jokes for years, even decades. Can you conceive of how soul-killing it must be to trot out the same lackluster material, night after night after night after night?

In candid interviews—usually given when they're too old to care—actors and comedians consistently refer to how much they loathe their audiences. The same goes for magicians, acrobats, clowns, public speakers, politicians, storytellers, game show hosts, vaudeville duos, seminarists, clergymen, lecturers, spiritual leaders, and celebrity stuntmen—every one of them.

But the audiences *don't know* this is how performers feel about them. If they did it would severely impede their enjoyment. Ignorance, you see, is the key to laughter.

?

More About Joking

Think of how tedious it is to listen to someone tell a long-winded joke you've heard dozens of times. Well what if that long-winded, tired joke was your life! What if every situation you faced, every person you met, every action you undertook had its end spelled out like the lame punchline at the end of a laborious, unfunny-even-the-first-time joke? Life would be intolerable.

Overtime

But now imagine a world which worked overtime to generate a steady stream of jokes of such originality, quality, and quantity that you never heard one a second time. And each one was better than the one that came before!

Imagine day after day with situations and people constantly—and unconsciously—conspiring to turn your life into an elaborate cosmic joke.

That's what living in true ignorance is like. By embracing the Power of Ignorance, you might find yourself so amused by everything in your life that you start laughing wildly and just . . . never stop!

?

Don't Tell Me How it Ends!

Isn't it so much less enjoyable to watch a movie when someone's spoiled the ending for you? Absolutely. That's why it's called "spoiled." Many people are so disenchanted with how much movie previews give away that they make a point of grumbling about it to their friends.

Isn't New

But this kind of thing isn't new.

Remember when you were a child, and you'd be watching a movie and your mother used to stop the film right near the end (or on those rare occasions when you went to the movie-theatre she'd hustle you out of the building) and thoughtfully tell you in detail about how the prince just didn't have the swordsmanship it took to defeat the dragon, and ended up defeated, decapitated, eaten, and humiliated, no matter how promising the earlier part of the film had been?

Remember how she wouldn't let you watch the end, instead describing the hero's death in gory detail, sparing you the torment of actually seeing it, softening the blow by keeping it in the reasonable confines of your young mind's imagination?

She did the same thing with the books you read, didn't she—snatching them out of your hands, giving you a full account of the hero's submission and slavery, and the wicked witch's cackling victory, before dropping those books into the woodstove.

Comfort

Sure, there was comfort in knowing how everything was going to turn out before even the hero did—as well as the comfort of how warm the burning books helped make the house.

Yes, it was nice not to be perched in suspense, forced to wonder if good would actually triumph, unlikely as it seemed.

But wasn't it nicer not to know they'd be stomped and savaged and have their ribs used as toothpicks?

Moments

Those moments before she sprang into the room there was always the hope that everything would work out. And even though you knew she'd be there soon enough to extinguish that hope like a firehose blasting out a spark, right before she did there were those two or three seconds when anything could happen. *Anything* . . . What a thrill that was!

Life is the same way.

Hopeful In Denver

I was recently sent this letter by a woman from somewhere in Colorado.

> Dearest Vaguen,
>
> I recently met a man who was giving a "cooking seminar" in my home town. Afterwards I introduced myself to him and we ended up talking for hours.
>
> Even though our time together was really brief, there was something there that we both wanted to keep hold of.
>
> I guess everyone's been hurt before and I'm no

different. But when I think of being with him I feel brave, that we might have something worth risking everything for.

After he left town we wrote to each other constantly and his letters were the most joyful thing in my day. They made me laugh, just like he did when we met. Even the thought that there might be one waiting for me would make me smile.

Then the letters stopped. And I don't know why. I do know that he's still feeling the sting of an old relationship gone bad and he's reticent to let that happen again, and I understand that.

What should I do? I know we could give each other a safe place to be real. But how do I tell him this without scaring him off even more?

Yours,

Hopeful in Denver

My Letter

Here's the letter I sent back to "Hopeful."

Dear "Hopeful,"

I'm heartily sorry to hear about your pain. I wish I could do more, but all I can offer you are the following thoughts.

Your man-friend reminds me of a friend of mine. Who is also a man. Let's say that my friend's name is . . . *Baguen*. He's a *jotivational* speaker who talks about the Power of *Imnorance*, while wearing a *burtleneck*.

Here's what my friend told me to tell you . . .

Poker

Imagine you're playing poker.

The cards are dealt, but before you can look at them you all have to go home.

You could still imagine that you were dealt the royal flush in spades, that you kept your poker face so well that you'd raised the pot, finally having a showdown with one other player, each of you certain of winning. The bets grew and grew just like the sexual tension until your opponent smugly revealed their royal flush in hearts. You played the moment perfectly, letting them think they'd won before suavely but not gloatingly revealing your own hand—a royal flush in spades. Then you discovered that all the other players had left. You laughed at yourselves for not noticing this, laughing so hard your glass of Tang spit out your nose. Laughing until finally the two of you were gasping for breath leaning against each other and you swept the cards off the table and . . . and . . .

Anyway, isn't that better than not having to go home, but instead picking up your measly pair of twos, substituting everything you can but faring no better, winding up broke and alone, forgotten at the end of the night, ignored by the two players who are making wild (yet tender and respectful) love on the table right in front of you?

Mother Movie Moment

Just like that moment before our mothers came in and ruined the movie, you've had a couple of months of hope. In your imagination of where things could have gone, you've experienced joy far greater than what you'd ever actually have known if you'd both continued this. And you've been spared the brutal torment of a relationship's inevitable decay and death throes.

If things weren't ended here, even those happy moments that you've already had would eventually be stripped of their value. And you'd look back on them as lies and find yourself wincing every time anything reminded you of them.

Man Feels

Maybe this man feels so strongly about you that he wants to spare you this. Maybe he needs to know that there's one person in the world who will remember him with affection. Maybe he agonized for hours wondering how to do this in the least painful way to you.

Not knowing that it hadn't failed is a lot better than *absolutely knowing* that it did, and having those memories like a millstone around your neck for the rest of your life.

Yours,

V

Think in Spanish

As you go about your lives pursuing ignorance in your own way it will be easy to fall into traps.

I was recently very excited when I saw signs all over my home town, advertising "Think in Spanish."

"That's a wonderful idea!" I thought, "I don't speak Spanish, so if I can think in it, I won't understand my own thoughts. What an amazing way for me to enhance my ignorance, whenever I need to."

I'm sure you can imagine my disappointment when I found out that it was actually a class that taught you how to speak *and* think in Spanish, and understand what it meant in English. I asked if there was some way to skip ahead to the thinking part, without being able to speak it or understand it, but the teacher just laughed at me, chasing me out of the school, telling me I was very handsome, and that I carried myself with grace.

A Note On Chapter 11

Some of you may have noticed that this book contains two chapter 11's.

If you didn't notice, then, well done.

But if you did, it's important that you know that you've failed. The lessons of ignorance have passed through your head without enhancing your life at all. Maybe you applied yourself too much. Maybe you weren't distracted enough. I suggest you buy another copy of this book and read it again. But don't try so hard.

Conclusion

If you've been reading this book in the correct order then you are approaching the end. We have journeyed together for as long as we can and it will soon be time for us to go our separate ways.

I'm sure if you were standing in front of me as I told you this you would say, "NO VAGUEN, DON'T LEAVE ME! I CAN'T DO THIS WITHOUT YOU! OHHHHHHHHH! WHY DOES EVERYONE I CARE ABOUT HAVE TO LEAVE? WHY? WHYYYYYYYY!!!???"

You would probably spend a little time pleading with me, trying to use logic to make me see that staying was in *my* best interests, but when that failed you would grab the lapels of my jacket and begin shaking roughly. Then you would realize that I wasn't wearing the jacket and therefore your shaking was only about half as threatening as it might be, so you would put it back on the chair before turning back to me. You would scream and point, threatening me with violence if I didn't stay, before collapsing to the floor, your body racked with sobs, where your pleading would become inarticulate. And as I turned to leave, my face betraying none of my own sorrow, but only my loving strength of will, you would clutch my leg in an iron grip and I would be forced to drag you around in the muck as I went about my daily routine.

Entertain The Possibility

After a certain length of time you would begin to entertain the possibility that you may be able to go on without me. You would realize that during our journey I had in fact taught you everything you needed to know to achieve Ignorance, and the wonderful life that comes with it, all by yourself. You would realize that you have the Igmantra; that you are familiar with Ignorant Breathing; that you have the means to inspire yourself using Ignorance, to give yourself real and imagined confidence. You would see that you can forget the knowledge that you can't possibly go on without me to guide you and as a result, you would begin to guide yourself.

But before we reach that point, there are a few final lessons which I need to teach you to ensure that you do not fall off the path as you take your first faltering newborn foal-like steps into a bigger world.

?

The Certificate of Ignorance

Many, many years ago I was studying with one of the great Igmasters. I asked him a question that had been troubling me for some time.

"How will I know when I've achieved Ignorance?"

He turned to me with an indulgent smile,

"How will you *know* when you've achieved Ignorance?"

"Yes." I replied.

"OK. Vaguen. I want you to think about the question you've just asked me."

"You do?"

"Yes. Think about the question, 'How will I know when I've achieved Ignorance?'"

"Well, if you're sure." I said, still uncertain that this wasn't some kind of trick.

Several minutes passed. I was soaked in sweat, and out of breath, but still no closer to an answer to my question. I told him so.

"Right" the Igmaster replied, "What was the fourth word of your question?"

"... um ... fourth word ... HOW!"

"No, that's the first word. What's the fourth word?"

"... Will?"

"That's the second word. You're not even trying to count are you?"

"No."

"That's right."

"What?"

He frowned, deep in thought. Finally he spoke again.

"Vaguen. You asked, 'How will you *know* when you've achieved ignorance?'"

I considered this for a while.

"Yes. Yes I *did* ask that. I remember. It was just now."

"Vaguen, 'How will you *know* when you've achieved ignorance?' Think about it."

". . ."

"'How will you KNOW when you've achieved ignorance?'"

". . ."

"'How will you . . . KNOW . . . when you've achieved ignorance?'"

". . ."

"'How will you . . . **KNOW** . . . when you've achieved ignorance?'"

". . ."

"Oh! For the love of dog!"

"Is it something to do with the word, *'know'*?" I asked.

"Yes! Yes it is, Vaguen! It's about *knowing* and *ignorance*. You know, I can honestly say that you are the biggest moron I have ever laid eyes on. I really have no idea how you've made it this far without dying."

I have never been so proud in all my life.

And I would like to have you, the reader(s) share in this pride.

The Certificate of Ignorance

So I have come up with the Certificate of Ignorance, a simple yet effective way to achieve the peace of mind that only knowing you're ignorant can bring.

You are undoubtedly asking, "HOW ME GET . . . CERTIFICATES OF IGNORANCE?"

It's simple. Just send a check for one thousand dollars to

"Vaguen" c/o the publisher and just one month later you will receive a bank statement telling you that the check has been cashed. Frame that bank statement and when you look at it you can be confident that you have achieved a level of ignorance few have ever dreamed of.

?

Recidivism

To really reap the benefits of ignorance you need to change habits that have lasted a lifetime. And this is not an easy thing to do.

All over the world people are trying to change their lives by altering their habits in this way; sticking to exercise regimes, maintaining diets, giving up smoking.

Statistics show that every sixty minutes in North America five hundred ex-smokers will pick up another cigarette. Think about that. Every hour, five hundred people. That means that just *in the time it has taken you to read this sentence another thousand people who were hoping to change their lives have begun smoking again.*

How do you avoid the perilous lure of slipping back into the life of knowledge?

It's actually very simple.

You must make a choice, a decision, every single day, for ignorance.

Difficult Decisions

Quite often in life we're faced with difficult decisions.

Let's say there's something we want to do, but we know a million reasons why it won't work. And why trying to make it work would only make things worse.

"You have to take a risk if you want your dreams to come true!" I hear you say.

That's a nice sentiment, but sometimes risks are dangerous.

That's why they're called risks. There are dangers out there that can break us in half.

Worth Taking

So how do we choose? Is the risk worth taking?

Consider this—not taking a risk can be just as dangerous.

So we see, it's not a choice between danger and safety, but a choice between *danger* and *other danger*.

Two Doors

Picture it this way.

There are two doors.

One leads to a room where someone *might* jab you with a fork. To death!

The other leads to a room in which you *will* freeze to death.

So how do you choose?

You don't have to. Why not just stay where you are? Corridors can be very nice places to be, and there are plenty of people in this world who would consider themselves very lucky to have one.

Except . . . Oh no! The corridor in which you're standing is on fire! The fire is creeping towards you, engulfing everything as it does. What about the other direction? No fire, but . . . there's a shape there! A figure. Huge. A hideous hulking shadow. It's turning very slowly, the hood is covering the face now, but you can see that there are eyes there; points of light reflecting in the fire that somehow speak of unspeakable evil. You don't want to look, but you can't help yourself. You're peering into that hood. You're transfixed as it reaches for you with its wooden spoon hands. But then you feel the heat of the fire as it gets closer. Well? Which door are you going to choose now? Are you going to be lonely forever thinking about what might have been? Or are you going to say "No! You were wrong mummy! I deserve to be happy! I can be happy! I can be loved! AND I'D RATHER RISK EVERYTHING FOR THAT THAN SETTLE FOR THIS MISERABLE SHAM OF AN EXISTENCE ONE DAY LONGER!"

About Vaguen

Vaguen is a successful motivational speaker and seminarist. As of this printing he is in the process of relocating to Denver, Colorado.

The Power of Ignorance
THE PLAY

TJ Dawe
and
Chris Gibbs

Based on original
material and characters
by Jeff Sumerel
and Sam Reynolds

Discover the play that started it all. *The Power of Ignorance: The Play* is a script not only for a smash-hit Fringe Festival play, but for your life. Make a commitment and join the few who understand the importance of understand that a lack of understanding is unimportant.

ISBN 1-897142-14-5 • $14.95 CDN / $12.95 US
WWW.BRINDLEANDGLASS.COM